TRAVESTIES

TRAVESTIES

TOM STOPPARD

GROVE PRESS
New York

Printed in the United States of America

Library of Congress Catalog Card Number 75-13552

ISBN: 978-0-8021-5089-9

Grove Press
an imprint of Grove/Atlantic, Inc.
154 West 14th Street
New York, NY 10011

Distributed by Publishers Group West

www.groveatlantic.com

16 17 18 19   29 28 27 26

For Oliver, Barnaby,
William and Edmund

The first performance of *Travesties* took place at the Aldwych Theatre, London, on 10 June 1974 in a production by the Royal Shakespeare Company. The cast was as follows:

HENRY CARR	John Wood
TRISTAN TZARA	John Hurt
JAMES JOYCE	Tom Bell
LENIN	Frank Windsor
BENNETT	John Bott
GWENDOLEN	Maria Aitken
CECILY	Beth Morris
NADYA	Barbara Leigh-Hunt

The play was directed by Peter Wood, and designed by Carl Toms with lighting by Robert Ornbo.

Travesties was revived by the Royal Shakespeare Company at the Barbican, London, on 16 October 1993 with the following cast:

HENRY CARR	Antony Sher
TRISTAN TZARA	David Westhead
JAMES JOYCE	Lloyd Hutchinson
LENIN	Geoffrey Freshwater
CECILY	Amanda Harris
GWENDOLEN	Rebecca Saire
BENNETT	Trevor Martin
NADYA	Darlene Johnson
Director	Adrian Noble
Designer	Richard Hudson
Lighting	Jennifer Tipton
Music	Guy Woolfenden

The text printed in this edition incorporates revisions made by the author for the above production.

Characters

HENRY CARR appears as a shabby and very old man and also as
   his youthful elegant self.

TRISTAN TZARA is the Dadaist of that name. He was a short,
   dark-haired, very boyish-looking young man, and charming
   (his word). He wears a monocle.

JAMES JOYCE is James Joyce in 1917/18, aged 36. He wears a
   jacket and trousers from two different suits.

LENIN is Lenin in 1917: aged 47.

BENNETT is Carr's manservant. Quite a weighty presence.

GWENDOLEN is Carr's younger sister; young and attractive but
   also a personality to be reckoned with.

CECILY is also young and attractive and even more to be reckoned
   with. Also appears as her old self.

NADYA is Nadezhda Krupskaya, Lenin's wife: aged 48.

Henry Wilfred Carr, 1894–1962

The reader of a play whose principal characters include Lenin, James Joyce and Tristan Tzara may not realize that the figure of Henry Carr is likewise taken from history. But this is so.

In March 1918 (I take the following information from Richard Ellmann's *James Joyce*), Claud Sykes, an actor temporarily living in Zurich, suggested to Joyce that they form a theatrical company to put on plays in English. Joyce agreed, and became the business manager of The English Players, the first production to be that of *The Importance of Being Earnest*. Actors were sought. Professionals were to receive a token fee of 30 francs and amateurs to make do with 10 francs for tram fare to rehearsals. Joyce became very active and visited the Consul General, A. Percy Bennett, in order to procure official approval for the Players. He succeeded in this, despite the fact that Bennett 'was annoyed with Joyce for not having reported to the Consulate officially to offer his services in wartime, and was perhaps aware of Joyce's work for the neutralist *International Review* and of his open indifference to the war's outcome. He may even have heard of Joyce's version of *Mr Dooley*, written about this time . . .' – I quote from Ellmann's superb biography, whose companionship was not the least pleasure in the writing of *Travesties*.

Meanwhile, Sykes was piecing together a cast . . . 'An important find was Tristan Rawson, a handsome man who had sung baritone roles for four years in the Cologne Opera House but had never acted in a play. After much coaxing Rawson agreed to take on the role of John Worthing. Sykes recruited Cecil Palmer as the butler, and found a woman named Ethel Turner to play Miss Prism . . . As yet, however, there was no one to take the leading role of Algernon Moncrieff. In an unlucky moment Joyce nominated a tall, goodlooking young man named Henry Carr, whom he had seen in the consulate. Carr, invalided from the service, had a small job there. Sykes learned that he had acted in some amateur plays in Canada, and decided to risk him.'

Carr's performance turned out to be a small triumph. He had

even, in his enthusiasm, bought some trousers, a hat and a pair of gloves to wear as Algernon. But immediately after the performance the actor and the business manager quarrelled. Joyce handed each member of the cast 10 or 30 francs, as pre-arranged, but succeeded in piquing Carr, who later complained to Sykes that Joyce had handed over the money like a tip.

The upshot was disproportionate and drawn out. Joyce and Carr ended up going to law, in two separate actions, Carr claiming reimbursement for the cost of the trousers, etc., or alternatively a share of the profits, and Joyce counter-claiming for the price of five tickets sold by Carr, and also suing for slander. These matters were not settled until February 1919. Joyce won on the money and lost on the slander, but he reserved his full retribution for *Ulysses*, where 'he allotted punishments as scrupulously and inexorably as Dante . . . Originally Joyce intended to make Consul General Bennett and Henry Carr the two drunken, blasphemous and obscene soldiers who knock Stephen Dedalus down in the "Circe" episode; but he eventually decided that Bennett should be the sergeant-major, with authority over Private Carr, who, however, refers to him with utter disrespect.'

From these meagre facts about Henry Carr – and being able to discover no others – I conjured up an elderly gentleman still living in Zurich, married to a girl he met in the Library during the Lenin years, and recollecting, perhaps not with entire accuracy, his encounters with Joyce and the Dadaist Tzara.

Soon after the play opened in London I was excited and somewhat alarmed to receive a letter beginning, 'I was totally fascinated by the reviews of your play – the chief reason being that Henry Carr was my husband until he died in 1962.' The letter was from Mrs Noël Carr, his second wife.

From her I learned that Henry Wilfred Carr was born in Sunderland in 1894 and brought up in County Durham. He was one of four sons, including his twin Walter, now also dead. At 17 Henry went to Canada where he worked for a time in a bank. In 1915 he volunteered for military service and went to France with the Canadian Black Watch. He was badly wounded the following year and – after lying five days in no-man's-land – was taken prisoner. Because of his wounds Henry was sent by the Germans to stay at a monastery where the monks tended him to a partial recovery, and then as an 'exchange prisoner' he was one of a group who were sent to Switzerland.

Thus Henry Carr arrived in Zurich where he was to cross the path of James Joyce and find himself a leading actor in both onstage and offstage dramas, leading to immortality of a kind as a minor character in *Ulysses*.

It was in Zurich, too, that he met his first wife, Nora Tulloch. They married in England after the war and later he took her back to Canada where he found a job in a department store in Montreal. He rose within the organization to become company secretary.

In 1928, while in Montreal, he met Noël Bach and after his divorce they were married there in 1933. The following year they returned to England. Henry ultimately joined a foundry company and when the next war came he and his wife were living in Sheffield. They were bombed out, and moved to a Warwickshire village, where Henry commanded the Home Guard, and they stayed in Warwickshire in the post-war years.

In 1962, while he was on a visit to London, Henry had a heart attack, and he died in St Mary Abbots Hospital, Kensington. He had no children.

I am indebted to Mrs Noël Carr for these biographical details, and, particularly, for her benevolence towards me and towards what must seem to her a peculiarly well-named play.

T.S.

Acknowledgements

Nearly everything spoken by Lenin and Nadezhda Krupskaya herein comes from his Collected Writings and from her *Memories of Lenin*. I have also profited variously – and gratefully – from the following books: *Lenin* by Michael C. Morgan; *Lenin* by Robert Payne; *Lenin and the Bolsheviks* by Adam B. Ulam; *To The Finland Station* by Edmund Wilson; *Days With Lenin* by Maxim Gorki; *The First World War, an Illustrated History* by A. J. P. Taylor; *James Joyce* by Richard Ellmann; *Joyce* by John Gross; *Dada, Art and Anti-Art* by Hans Richter; and *The Dada Painters and Poets*, edited by Robert Motherwell. I am also indebted to Mr James Klugmann for material relating to Lenin in Switzerland. The responsibility for the use to which this and all other material is put is my own.

ACT ONE

The play is set in Zurich, in two locations: the drawing room of Henry Carr's apartment ('THE ROOM'), and a section of the Zurich Public Library ('THE LIBRARY'). Most of the action takes place within Carr's memory, which goes back to the period of the First World War, and this period is reflected appropriately in the design and the costumes, etc. It is to be supposed that Old Carr has lived in the same apartment since that time.

The ROOM must have the main door Centre Upstage: most of the entrances would be weakened seriously if they occurred from the side. Double doors would be best. However, there is also at least one side door. There is a centre table with a good chair on each side, and a side table, apart from other furniture.

The LIBRARY suggests a larger scale – tall bookcases, etc. In Act Two Cecily (the librarian) requires a counter or desk, which need not necessarily be in view at the beginning of the play. Some of the entrances, e.g. Nadya's, are probably through a door rather than from the wings.

The LIBRARY in the Prologue and the Second Act does not necessarily have to be presented from the same angle.

We begin in the LIBRARY

There are places for JOYCE, LENIN and TZARA.

GWEN sits with JOYCE. They are occupied with books, papers, pencils . . .

LENIN is also writing quietly, among books and papers. TZARA is writing as the play begins. On his table are a hat and a large pair of scissors. TZARA finishes writing, then takes up the scissors and cuts the paper, word by word, into his hat. When all the words are in the hat he shakes the hat and empties it on the table. He rapidly separates the bits of paper into random lines, turning a few over, etc., and then reads the result in a loud voice.

I

TZARA: Eel ate enormous appletzara
   key dairy chef's hat he'll learn oomparah!
   Ill raced alas whispers kill later nut east,
   noon avuncular ill day Clara!
CECILY (*Entering*): Sssssssh!
   (*Her admonition is to the Library in general. She enters from one
   wing, not through the door, and crosses the stage, leaving by the
   opposite wing, moving quite quickly, like someone who is busy.
   No one takes any notice.*)
JOYCE (*Dictating to* GWEN): Deshill holles eamus . . .
GWEN (*Writing*): Deshill holles eamus . . .
JOYCE: Thrice.
GWEN: Uh-hum.
JOYCE: Send us bright one, light one, Horhorn, quickening and
   wombfruit.
GWEN: Send us bright one, light one, Horhorn, quickening and
   wombfruit.
JOYCE: Thrice.
GWEN: Uh-hum.
JOYCE: Hoopsa, boyaboy, hoopsa!
GWEN: Hoopsa, boyaboy, hoopsa!
JOYCE: Hoopsa, boyaboy, hoopsa!
GWEN: Likewise thrice?
JOYCE: Uh-hum.
   (*By this time* TZARA *has replaced the bits of paper into the hat.
   He takes out a handful, and reads the words one at a time,
   placing them into the hat as he reads each one.*)
TZARA: Clara avuncular!
   Whispers ill oomparah!
   Eel nut dairy day
   Appletzara . . .
   . . . Hat!
CECILY (*Re-entering*): Ssssssh!
   (CECILY *has come in with a few books which she places by*
   LENIN.)
   (TZARA *leaves the Library through the door.*)
   (*It is now necessary that the audience should observe the
   following:* GWEN *has received from* JOYCE *a folder.* CECILY

2

receives an identical folder from LENIN. *These folders, assumed
to contain manuscripts, are eye-catching objects in some striking
colour. Each girl has cause to place her folder down on a table or
chair, and each girl then picks up the wrong folder. In the
original production,* GWEN *dropped a glove, etc., etc., but it is
not important how this transference is achieved, only that it is
seen to occur.*)
(GWEN *is now ready to leave the Library, and does so, taking
Lenin's folder with her.*)
(CECILY *also leaves, not through the door but into the wings.*)
(NADYA *enters as* GWEN *leaves; they bump into each other, and
each apologizes,* GWEN *in English,* NADYA *in Russian.*)
(NADYA *enters in an agitated state. She looks round for her
husband and goes straight to him. Their conversation is in
Russian.*)

NADYA: Vylodya!

LENIN: Shto takoya? (*What is it?*)

NADYA: Bronsky prishol. On s'kazal shto v'Peterburge revolutsia!
(*Bronsky came to the house. He says there's a revolution in St
Petersburg.*)

LENIN: Revolutsia!
(*At this point* JOYCE *stands up and begins to walk up and down
searching his pockets for tiny scraps of paper on which he has
previously written down things he may wish to use. While the
Lenins continue their conversation,* JOYCE *fishes out, one by one,
these scraps of paper and reads out what he finds on them.*)

JOYCE (*Regarding his first find*): 'Morose delectation . . . Aquinas
tunbelly . . . Frate porcospino . . .'
(*He decides he doesn't need this one. He screws it up and throws
it away, and finds a second . . .*)
'Und alle Schiffe brucken . . .'
(*He decides to keep this one, so re-pockets it. He takes out
another.*)
'Entweder transubstantiality, oder consubstantiality, but in
no way substantiality . . .'
(*He decides to keep this one as well. Meanwhile, the* LENINS
have been continuing in the following manner):

LENIN: Otkuda on znayet? (*How does he know?*)

3

NADYA: Napisano v'Gazetakh. On govorit shto Tsar sobiraet'sia otretchsya ot prestola! (*It's all in the papers. He says the Tsar is going to abdicate!*)

LENIN: Shtoty! (*No!*)

NADYA: Da! (*Yes!*)

LENIN: Eto v'gazetakh? (*Is that in the newspapers?*)

NADYA: Da – da. Idiom damoi. On zhdyot. (*Yes – yes. Come on home. He's waiting.*)

LENIN: On tam? (*Is he there?*)

NADYA: Da! (*Yes!*)

LENIN: Gazetakh u nievo? (*He brought the paper?*)

NADYA: Da! (*Yes!*)

LENIN: Ty sama vidyela? (*You saw it yourself?*)

NADYA: Da, da, da! (*Yes, yes, yes!*)

> (JOYCE's *voice, however, has dominated this passage. He now encounters a further scrap of paper which is lying on the floor:* LENIN *has inadvertently dropped it.* JOYCE *picks this paper up.* NADYA *is leaving the Library, through the door,* LENIN *saying in Russian . . .*)

LENIN: Idyi nazad y skazhee y'moo shto ya prichazhoo. Tolka sobieru svayi b'magi. (*Go home ahead of me. I will collect my papers and follow.*)

> (LENIN *is gathering his papers.* JOYCE *is examining the dropped paper.*)

JOYCE: 'Lickspittle – capitalist – lackeys – of imperialism.'

> (LENIN *recognizes these words. He pauses, and approaches* JOYCE.)

LENIN: Pardon! . . . Entschuldigung! . . . Scusi! . . . Excuse me!

JOYCE (*Handing him the paper*): Je vous en prie! Bitte! Prego! It's perfectly all right!

> (LENIN *leaves.* JOYCE *is alone now.*)
> (*Declaims*) A librarianness of Zurisssh
> only emerged from her niche
> when a lack of response
> to *Nicht Reden! Silence!*
> obliged her to utter the plea –

CECILY (*Entering as before*): – ssssssh!

> (JOYCE *accedes to her request, puts on his hat, picks up his stick,*

and while she regards him with disapproval he leaves at a strolling pace, singing . . .)

JOYCE: If you ever go across the sea to Ireland . . .

It may be at the closing of the day . . .

You can sit and watch the moon rise over Claddagh

and watch the sun go down on Galway Bay . . .

(The stage now belongs to OLD CARR. *The* LIBRARY *must now be replaced by the* ROOM. *Needless to say, the change should occur with as little disruption as possible, and the use of music as a bridge is probably desirable.)*

(NOTE: In the original production, the Room contained a piano which was at different times used by Old Carr, and in this instance Old Carr played (very badly) the tune of Galway Bay while the set was changed; the piano being right downstage in a permanent position. It is possible that CARR *has been immobile on stage from the beginning, an old man remembering . . .)*

CARR: He was Irish, of course. Though not actually from Limerick – he was a Dublin man, Joyce, everybody knows that, couldn't have written the book without. There was a young man from Dublin, tum-ti-ti-tum-ti-ti troublin' . . . I used to have quite a knack for it, but there's little encouragement for that sort of thing in the Consular Service. Not a great patron of poetry, the Service, didn't push it, never made a feature of it. I mean you'd never say that a facility for rhyme and metre was the sine qua non of advancement in the Consular Service . . . Didn't *dis*courage it, I'm not saying that, on the contrary, a most enlightened and cultivated body of men, fully sympathetic to all the arts (look no further than the occasion that brought us together, me and Joyce, brought him to this room, full support, a theatrical event of the first water, great success, personal triumph in the demanding role of Ernest, not Ernest, the other one, in at the top, have we got the cucumber sandwiches for Lady Bracknell, notwithstanding the unfortunate consequences. Irish lout. Not one to bear a grudge, however, not after all these years, and him dead in the cemetery up the hill, no hard feelings either side, unpleasant as it is to be dragged through the courts for a few francs (though it wasn't the money, or the trousers for that matter), *but*, be that as it may, all in all, truth be told, the encouragement of poetry writing was not the primary concern of the British Consulate in Zurich in 1917, and now I've lost my knack for it. Too late to go back for it. Alas and alack for it. But I digress. No apologies required, constant digression being the saving grace of senile reminiscence.

My memoirs, is it, then? Life and times, friend of the famous. Memories of James Joyce. James Joyce As I Knew Him. The James Joyce I Knew. Through the Courts With James Joyce . . . What was he like, James Joyce, I am often asked. It is true that I knew him well at the height of his powers, his genius in full flood in the making of *Ulysses*, before publication and fame turned him into a public monument for pilgrim cameras more often than not in a velvet smoking jacket of an unknown colour, photography being in those days a black and white affair, but probably real blue if not empirical purple and sniffing a bunch of sultry violets that positively defy development, don't go on, do it on my head, caviar for the general public, now then – *Memories of James Joyce* . . . It's coming.

To those of us who knew him, Joyce's genius was never in doubt. To be in his presence was to be aware of an amazing intellect bent on shaping itself into the permanent form of its own monument – the book the world now knows as *Ulysses*! Though at that time we were still calling it (I hope memory serves) by its original title, Elasticated Bloomers.

A prudish, prudent man, Joyce, in no way profligate or vulgar, and yet convivial, without being spend-thrift, and yet still without primness towards hard currency in all its transmutable and transferable forms and denominations, of which, however, he demanded only a sufficiency from the world at large, exhibiting a monkish unconcern for worldly and bodily comforts, without at the same time shutting himself off from the richness of human society, whose temptations, on the other hand, he met with an ascetic disregard tempered only by sudden and catastrophic aberrations – in short, a complex personality, an enigma, a

6

contradictory spokesman for the truth, an obsessive litigant and yet an essentially private man who wished his total indifference to public notice to be universally recognized – in short a liar and a hypocrite, a tight-fisted, sponging, fornicating drunk not worth the paper, that's that bit done.

Further recollections of a Consular Official in Whitest Switzerland. The Ups and Downs of Consular Life in Zurich During the Great War: A Sketch.

'Twas in the bustling metropolis of swiftly gliding trams and greystone banking houses, of cosmopolitan restaurants on the great stone banks of the swiftly-gliding snot-green (mucus mutandis) Limmat River, of jewelled escapements and refugees of all kinds, e.g. Lenin, there's a point . . . Lenin As I Knew Him. The Lenin I Knew. Halfway to the Finland Station with V. I. Lenin: A Sketch. I well remember the first time I met Lenin, or as he was known on his library ticket, Vladimir Ilyich Ulyanov. To be in his presence was to be aware of a complex personality, enigmatic, magnetic, but not, I think, astigmatic, his piercing brown (if memory serves) eyes giving no hint of it. An essentially simple man, and yet an intellectual theoretician, bent, as I was already aware, on the seemingly impossible task of reshaping the civilized world into a federation of standing committees of workers' deputies. As I shook the hand of this dynamic, gnomic and yet not, I think, anaemic stranger, who with his fine head of blond hair falling over his forehead had the clean-shaven look of a Scandinavian seafaring – hello, hello, got the wrong chap, has he? – take no notice, all come out in the wash, that's the art of it. Fact of the matter, *who* (without benefit of historical perspective and the photograph album, Red Square packed to the corner stickers with comraderaderie, and now for our main speaker, balding bearded in the three-piece suit, good God if it isn't Ulyanov!, knew him well, always sat between the window and Economics A–K etceterarera) well, take away all *that*, and who was he to Radek or Radek to him, or Martov or Martinov, Plekhanov, or he to Ulyanov for that matter? – in Zurich in 1917? Café conspirators, so what? Snowballs in hell. Snowballs at all, Lenin he only had one chance in a million,

7

remember the time they had the meeting? – Social
Democrats for Civil War in Europe. Total attendance: four.
Ulyanov, Mrs Ulyanov, Zinoviev and a police spy. And now
they want to know what was he like? What was he like,
Lenin, I am often asked.
(*He makes an effort*).
To those of us who knew him Lenin's greatness was never in
doubt.
(*He gives up again.*)
So why didn't you put a pound on him, you'd be a
millionaire, like that chap who bet sixpence against the
Titanic. No. Truth of the matter, who'd have thought big
oaks from a corner room at number 14 Spiegelgasse? – now
here's a thing: two revolutions formed *in the same street*. Face
to face in Spiegelgasse! *Street of Revolution! A sketch*. Meet
by the sadly-sliding chagrinned Limmat River, strike west
and immediately we find ourselves soaking wet, strike east
and immediately we find ourselves in the Old Town, having
left behind the banking bouncing metropolis of trampolines
and chronometry of all kinds for here time has stopped in the
riddled maze of alleyways and by the way you'd never believe
a Swiss redlight district, pornographic fretwork shops, vice
dens, get a grip on yourself, sorry, sorry, second right, third
left – Spiegelgasse! – narrow, cobbled, high old houses in a
solid rank, number 14 the house of the narrow cobbler
himself, Kammerer his name, Lenin his tenant – and across
the way at Number One, the Meierei Bar, crucible of anti-
art, cradle of Dada!!! Who? What? Whatsisay Dada?? You
remember Dada! – historical halfway house between
Futurism and Surrealism, twixt Marinetti and André
Breton, 'tween the before-the-war-to-end-all-wars years and
the between-the-wars years – *Dada*! – down with reason,
logic, causality, coherence, tradition, proportion, sense and
consequence, my art belongs to Dada 'cos Dada 'e treats me
so – well then, *Memories of Dada by a Consular Friend of the
Famous in Old Zurich: A Sketch*.
    What did it do in the Great War, Dada, I am often asked.
How did it begin? where did it? when? what was it, who

named it and why Dada? These are just some of the questions that continue to baffle Dadaists the world over. To those of us who lived through it Dada was, topographically speaking, the high point of Western European culture – I well remember as though it were yesteryear (oh where are they now?) how Hugo Ball – or was it Hans Arp? yes! – no – Picabia, was it? – no, Tzara – yes! – wrote his name in the snow with a walking stick and said: There! I think I'll call it The Alps. Oh the yes-no's of yesteryear. Whose only age done gone. Over the hills and far away the sixpounders pounding in howitzerland, no louder than the soft thud of snow falling off the roof – *oh heaven!* to be picked out – plucked out – blessed by the blood of a negligible wound and released into the folds of snow-covered hills – Oh, Switzerland! – unfurled like a white flag, pacific civilian Switzerland – the miraculous neutrality of it, the non-combatant impartiality of it, the non-aggression pacts of it, the international red cross of it – entente to the left, détente to the right, into the valley of the invalided blundered and wandered myself when young –

Carr of the Consulate! – first name Henry, that much is beyond dispute, I'm mentioned in the books.

For the rest I'd be willing to enter into discussion but not if you don't mind correspondence, into matters of detail and chronology – I stand open to correction on all points, except for my height which can't be far off, and the success of my performance, which I remember clearly, in the demanding role of Ernest (not Ernest, the other one) – *that*, and the sense of sheer relief at arriving in a state of rest, namely Switzerland, the still centre of the wheel of war. That's really the thing –
(CARR *is now a young man in his drawing room in 1917. Ideally the actor should simply take off e.g. a hat and dressing gown – no wig or beard, no make-up – Carr's age has been in his voice.*)
– the first thing to grasp about Switzerland is that there is no war here. Even when there is war *everywhere else*, there is no war in Switzerland.
BENNETT: Yes, sir.
(BENNETT *has entered with a tray of tea things, set for two, with sandwiches.*)

9

CARR: It is this complete absence of bellicosity, coupled with an ostentatious punctuality of public clocks, that gives the place its reassuring air of permanence. Switzerland, one instinctively feels, will not go away. Nor will it turn into somewhere else. You have no doubt heard allusions to the beneficial quality of the Swiss air, Bennett. The quality referred to is permanence.

BENNETT: Yes, sir.

CARR: Desperate men who have heard the clocks strike thirteen in Alsace, in Trieste, in Serbia and Montenegro, who have felt the ground shift beneath them in Estonia, Austro-Hungary and the Ottoman Empire, arrive in Switzerland and after a few deep breaths find that the ringing and buzzing in their ears has regulated itself into a soothing tick-tock, and that the ground beneath their feet, while invariably sloping, is as steady as an alp. Tonight I incline to the theatre; get me out the straight cut trouser with the blue satin stripe and the silk cutaway. I'll wear the opal studs.

BENNETT: Yes, sir. I have put the newspapers and telegrams on the sideboard, sir.

CARR: Is there anything of interest?

BENNETT: The *Neue Zuricher Zeitung* and the *Zuricher Post* announce, respectively, an important Allied and German victory, each side gaining ground after inflicting heavy casualties on the other with little loss to itself.

CARR: Ah – yes . . . the war! Poor devils! How I wish I could get back to the trenches! – to my comrades in arms – the wonderful spirit out there in the mud and wire – the brave days and fearful nights. Bliss it was to see the dawn! To be alive was very heaven! Never in the whole history of human conflict was there anything to match the carnage – God's blood!, the shot and shell! – graveyard stench! – Christ Jesu! – deserted by simpletons, they damn us to hell – ora pro nobis – quick! no, *get me out*! – I think to match the carnation, oxblood shot-silk cravat, starched, creased just so, asserted by a simple pin, the damask lapels – or a brown, no, biscuit – no – get me out the straight cut trouser with the blue satin stripe and the silk cutaway. I'll wear the opal studs.

BENNETT: Yes, sir. I have put the newspapers and telegrams on the
sideboard, sir.

CARR: Is there anything of interest?

BENNETT: The war continues to dominate the newspapers, sir.

CARR: Ah yes . . . the war, always the war . . .

*(A note on the above: the scene (and most of the play) is under the
erratic control of Old Carr's memory, which is not notably reliable,
and also of his various prejudices and delusions. One result is that
the story (like a toy train perhaps) occasionally jumps the rails and
has to be restarted at the point where it goes wild.*

*This scene has several of these 'time slips', indicated by the
repetitions of the exchange between* BENNETT *and* CARR *about the
'newspapers and telegrams'. Later in the play there are similar
cycles as Carr's memory drops a scene and then picks it up again
with a repeated line (e.g.* CARR *and* CECILY *in the Library). It
may be desirable to mark these moments more heavily by using an
extraneous sound or a light effect, or both. The sound of a
cuckoo-clock, artificially amplified, would be appropriate since it
alludes to time and to Switzerland; in which case a naturalistic
cuckoo-clock could be seen to strike during the here-and-now scene
of Old Carr's first monologue. At any rate the effect of these
time-slips is not meant to be bewildering, and it should be made
clear what is happening.)*

I was in Savile Row when I heard the news, talking to the head
cutter at Drewitt and Madge in a hounds-tooth check slightly
flared behind the knee, quite unusual. Old Drewitt, or
Madge, came in and told me. Never trusted the Hun, I
remarked. Boche, he replied, and I, at that time unfamiliar
with the appellation, turned on my heel and walked into
Trimmett and Punch where I ordered a complete suit of
Harris knicker-bockers with hacking vents. By the time they
were ready, I was in France. Great days! Dawn breaking over
no-man's-land. Dewdrops glistening on the poppies in the
early morning sun – All quiet on the Western Front . . .
Tickety boo, tickety boo, tickety boo . . .

BENNETT: A gentleman called, sir. He did not wait.

CARR: What did he want?

BENNETT: He did not vouchsafe his business, sir. He left his card.

(*Offers it on a salver.*)

CARR: 'Tristan Tzara. Dada Dada Dada.' Did he have a stutter?

BENETT: He spoke French with a Romanian accent, and wore a monocle.

CARR: He is obviously trying to pass himself off as a spy. It is a form of vanity widely indulged in in Zurich during a European war, I believe, and adds greatly to the inconveniences caused by the crowds of *real* spies who conspire to fill the Odeon and the Terrasse, and make it almost impossible to get a table at either.

BENNETT: I have noticed him with a group of friends at the Terrasse, sir. Whether they were conspirators I could not, of course, tell.

CARR: To masquerade as a conspirator, or at any rate to speak French with a Romanian accent and wear a monocle, is at least as wicked as to be one; in fact, rather more wicked, since it gives a dishonest impression of perfidy, and, moreover, makes the over-crowding in the cafés gratuitous, being the result neither of genuine intrigue nor bona fide treachery – was it not, after all, La Rochefoucauld in his *Maximes* who had it that in Zurich in Spring in wartime a gentleman is hard put to find a vacant seat for the spurious spies peeping at police spies spying on spies eyeing counter-spies *what a bloody country even the cheese has got holes in it!!* (*Off the rails again.* CARR *has, on the above words, done violence to the inside of a cheese sandwich.*)

BENNETT: Yes, sir. I have put the newspapers and telegrams on the sideboard, sir.

CARR: Is there anything of interest?

BENNETT: There is a revolution in Russia, sir.

CARR: Really? What sort of revolution?

BENNETT: A social revolution, sir.

CARR: A *social* revolution? Unaccompanied women smoking at the Opera, that sort of thing? . . .

BENNETT: Not precisely that, sir. It is more in the nature of a revolution of classes contraposed by the fissiparous disequilibrium of Russian society.

CARR: What do you mean, classes?

BENNETT: Masters and servants. As it were. Sir.

CARR: Oh. Masters and servants. *Classes.*

BENNETT (*Expressionless as always*): There have been scenes of violence.

CARR: I see. Well, I'm not in the least bit surprised, Bennett. I don't wish to appear wise after the event, but anyone with half an acquaintance with Russian society could see that the day was not far off before the exploited class, disillusioned by the neglect of its interests, alarmed by the falling value of the rouble, and above all goaded beyond endurance by the insolent rapacity of its servants, should turn upon those butlers, footmen, cooks, valets . . . Parenthetically, Bennett, I see from your book that on Thursday night when Mr Tzara was dining with me, eight bottles of champagne are entered as having been consumed. I have had previous occasion to speak to you of the virtues of moderation, Bennett: this time I will only say, remember Russia.

BENNETT: Yes, sir. I have put the newspapers and telegrams on the sideboard, sir.

CARR: Is there anything of interest?

BENNETT: The Tsar has now abdicated, sir. There is a Provisional Government headed by Prince Lvov, with Guchkov as Minister of War, Milyukov Foreign Minister and the Socialist Kerensky as Minister of Justice. The inclusion of Kerensky is calculated to recommend the Government to a broad base of the common people, but effective authority has already been challenged by a committee of workers' deputies, or 'Soviet', which has for the moment united all shades of socialist opinion. However there is no immediate prospect of the Socialists seizing power, for the revolution is regarded by them as the fulfilment of Karl Marx's prophecy of a *bourgeois capitalist era* in Russia's progress towards socialism. According to Marx, there is no way for a country to leap from autocracy to socialism: while the *ultimate* triumph of socialism is inevitable, being the necessary end of the process of dialectical materialism, it must be preceded by a bourgeois-capitalist stage of development. When the time is ripe, and not before, there will be a further revolution, led by the organized industrial workers, or 'Proletariat'. Thus, it is the duty of Russian Marxists to welcome the present bourgeois revolution, even though it might take several generations to get through. As things stand, therefore, if one can be certain of anything it is that Russia is set fair to become a parliamentary democracy on the British model.

CARR: Newspapers or coded telegram?

BENNETT: General rumour put about Zurich by the crowds of spies, counter-spies, radicals, artists and riff-raff of all kinds. Mr Tzara called, sir. He did not wait.

CARR: I'm not sure that I approve of your taking up this modish novelty of 'free association', Bennett.

BENNETT: I'm sorry, sir. It is only that Mr Tzara being an artist –

CARR: I will not have you passing moral judgements on my friends. If Mr Tzara is an artist that is his misfortune.

BENNETT: Yes, sir. I have put the newspapers and telegrams on the sideboard, sir.

CARR: Is there anything of interest?

BENNETT: In St Petersburg, the Provisional Government has now declared its intention to carry on the war. However, the committee of workers' deputies, or Soviet, consider the war to be nothing more than an imperialist adventure carried on at the expense of workers of both sides. To co-operate in this adventure is to be stigmatized in a novel phrase which seems to translate as a 'lickspittle capitalist lackey', unnecessarily offensive in my view.

CARR (*Languidly*): I'm not sure that I'm much interested in your views, Bennett.

BENNETT (*Apologetically*): They're *not* particularly interesting, sir. However, there is a more extreme position put forward by the Bolshevik party. The Bolshevik line is that some unspecified but unique property of the Russian situation, unforeseen by Marx, has caused the bourgeois-capitalist era of Russian history to be compressed into the last few days, and that the time for the proletarian revolution is now ripe. But the Bolsheviks are a small minority in the Soviet, and their leader, Vladimir Ulyanov, also known as Lenin, has been in exile since the abortive 1905 revolution, and is in fact living in Zurich.

CARR: Naturally.

BENNETT: Yes, sir – if I may quote La Rochefoucauld, 'Quel pays sanguinaire, même le fromage est plein des trous.' Lenin is desperately trying to return to Russia but naturally the Allies will not allow him free passage. Since Lenin is almost alone in proclaiming the Bolshevik orthodoxy, which is indeed his creation, his views at present count for nothing in St Petersburg. A betting man would lay odds of about a million to one against Lenin's view prevailing. However, it is suggested that you take all steps to ascertain his plans.

CARR: I ascertain Lenin's plans?

BENNETT: Telegram from the Minister.

(*He starts to leave.*)

CARR: A million to one.

BENNETT: I'd put a pound on him, sir.

CARR: You know him?

BENNETT: I do, sir. And if any doubt remained, the British Secret Service assures us that the man to watch is Kerensky.

(*Exit* BENNETT.)

CARR (*Aside*): Bennett seems to be showing alarming signs of irony. I have always found that irony among the lower orders is the first sign of an awakening social consciousness. It remains to be seen whether it will grow into an armed seizure of the means of production, distribution and exchange, or spend itself in liberal journalism.

BENNETT (*Entering*): Mr Tzara.

(TZARA *enters.* BENNETT *retires.*)

CARR: How are you, my dear Tristan. What brings you here?

(*This Tzara (there is to be another) is a Romanian nonsense. His entrance might be set to appropriate music.*)

TZARA (*Ebulliently*): Plaizure, plaizure! What else? Eating ez usual, I see 'Enri?! – 'allo – 'allo, vhat is all the teapots etcetera? Somebody cominck? It is Gwendolen I hopp! – I luff 'er, 'Enri – I have come by tram expressly to propose a marriage – ah – ha! –

BENNETT (*Entering*): Miss Gwendolen and Mr Joyce.

15

(GWENDOLEN and JAMES JOYCE enter. BENNETT remains by the door. GWENDOLEN and TZARA are momentarily transfixed by each other. This is hardly noticed as JOYCE has made it his own entrance.)

JOYCE: Top o' the morning! – James Joyce!
I hope you'll allow me to voice
my regrets in advance
for coming on the off-chance –
b'jasus I hadn't much choice!

(This JOYCE is obviously an Irish nonsense. The whole scene is going to take a limerick form, so for clarity's sake the lay-out of the text is modified.)

CARR: I . . . sorry . . . would you say that again?

JOYCE: Begob – I'd better explain
I'm told that you are a –

TZARA: Miss Carr!

GWEN: Mr Tzara!

JOYCE: *(Seeing TZARA for the first time)* B'jasus'. Joyce is the
name.

GWEN: I'm sorry! – how terribly rude!
Henry – Mr Joyce!

CARR: How d'you do?

JOYCE: Delighted!

TZARA: Good day!

JOYCE: I just wanted to say
how sorry I am to intrude.

CARR: Tell me . . . are you some kind of a poet?

JOYCE: You know my work?

CARR: No – it's
something about your deliv'ry –
can't quite –

JOYCE: Irish.

CARR: From Lim'rick?

JOYCE: No – Dublin, don't tell me you know it!

GWEN: He's a poor writer –

JOYCE: Aha!
A fine writer who writes caviar
for the general, hence poor –

16

TZARA:	Wants to touch you for sure.
JOYCE:	I'm addressing my friend, Mr . . .
CARR:	(*Gulp*) Carr.
GWEN:	Mr Tzara writes poetry and sculpts,
	with quite unexpected results.
	I'm told he recites
	and on Saturday nights
	does all kinds of things for adults.
JOYCE:	I really don't think Mr Carr
	is interested much in da-dah –
TZARA:	We say it like Dah-da.
JOYCE:	(*To* CARR) The fact is I'm rather
	hard up.
CARR:	Yes I'm told that you are.
	If it's money you want, I'm afraid . . .
GWEN:	Oh, Henry! – he's mounting a play,
	and Mr Joyce thought
	your official support . . .
CARR:	Ah . . .!
JOYCE:	And a couple of pounds till I'm paid.
CARR:	I don't see why not. For my part,
	H.M.G. is considered pro-Art.
TZARA:	Consider me anti.
GWEN:	Consider your auntie?
JOYCE:	A pound would do for a start.
CARR:	The Boche put on culture a-plenty
	for Swiss, what's the word?
JOYCE:	Cognoscenti.
CARR:	It's worth fifty tanks
JOYCE:	Or twenty-five francs
CARR:	Now . . . British culture . . .
JOYCE:	I'll take twenty.
TZARA:	(*Scornful*) Culture and reason!
JOYCE:	Fifteen.
TZARA:	They give us the mincing machine!
GWEN:	That's awf'ly profound.
JOYCE:	Could you lend me a pound?
TZARA:	All literature is obscene!

The classics – tradition – vomit on it!
GWEN: (Oh!)
TZARA: Beethoven! Mozart! I spit on it!
GWEN: (Oh!)
TZARA: Everything's chance!
GWEN: Consider your aunts.
TZARA: Causality – logic – I sssssh –
GWEN: – awf'ly profound
JOYCE: (*To* BENNETT) Could you lend me a pound?
GWEN: I thought he was going to say 'Shit on it'.
(*Her hand flies, too late, to her mouth.* CARR *has been thinking hard.*)
CARR: By jove, I've got it! *Iolanthe!*
TZARA: Obscene!
CARR: 　　　　Is it?
TZARA: 　　　　　　Avanti!
Gut'n tag! Adios!
GWEN: Au revoir!
TZARA: Vamonos!
BENNETT: Give my regards to your auntie.
(BENNETT *closes the door behind* TZARA *and* GWEN.)
(*The whole thing has been manic from beginning to end, and now it's finished, except that* JOYCE *is a leftover.*)
JOYCE: A Romanian rhymer I met
used a system he based on roulette.
His reliance on chance
was a def'nite advance
and yet . . . and yet . . . and yet . . .
(*The light steps down between verses.*)
An impromptu poet of Hibernia
rhymed himself into a hernia.
He became quite adept
at the practice except
for occasional anti-climaxes.

When I want to leave things in the air
I say, 'Excuse me, I've got to repair
to my book about Bloom –'

18

and just leave the room.

(*He has gone. Pause. Low light on motionless* CARR *in his chair.*)

CARR: Well, let us resume. *Zurich By One Who Was There.*
  (*Normal light.*)

BENNETT (*entering*): Mr Tzara.
  (TZARA *enters.* BENNETT *retires.*)

CARR: How are you, my dear Tristan? What brings you here?
  (TZARA, *no less than* CARR, *is straight out of* The Importance
  of Being Earnest.)

TZARA: Oh, pleasure, pleasure! What else should bring anyone
  anywhere? Eating and drinking, as usual, I see, Henry? I
  have often observed that Stoical principles are more easily
  borne by those of Epicurean habits.

CARR (*Stiffly*): I believe it is done to drink a glass of hock and
  seltzer before luncheon, and it is well done to drink it well
  before luncheon. I took to drinking hock and seltzer for my
  nerves at a time when nerves were fashionable in good
  society. This season it is trenchfoot, but I drink it regardless
  because I feel much better after it.

TZARA: You might have felt much better anyway.

CARR: No, no -- post hock, propter hock.

TZARA: But, my dear Henry, causality is no longer fashionable
  owing to the war.

CARR: How illogical, since the war itself had causes. I forget what
  they were, but it was all in the papers at the time. Something
  about brave little Belgium, wasn't it?

TZARA: Was it? I thought it was Serbia . . .

CARR: Brave little Serbia . . .? No, I don't think so. The
  newspapers would never have risked calling the British
  public to arms without a proper regard for succinct
  alliteration.

TZARA: Oh, what nonsense you talk!

CARR: It may be nonsense, but at least it is clever nonsense.

TZARA: I am sick of cleverness. In point of fact, everything is
  Chance.

CARR: That sounds awfully clever. What does it mean?

TZARA: It means, my dear Henry, that the causes we know

everything about depend on causes we know very little about, which depend on causes we know absolutely nothing about. And it is the duty of the artist to jeer and howl and belch at the delusion that infinite generations of real effects can be inferred from the gross expression of apparent cause.

CARR: It is the duty of the artist to beautify existence.

TZARA (*Articulately*): Dada dada dada dada dada dada dada dada dada dada dada dada dada dada dada dada dada dada dada dada dada dada dada dada dada dada dada dada dada dada dada dada dada dada dada.

CARR (*Slight pause*): Oh, what nonsense you talk!

TZARA: It may be nonsense, but at least it's not clever nonsense. Cleverness has been exploded, along with so much else, by the war.

CARR: You forget that I was there, in the mud and blood of a foreign field, unmatched by anything in the whole history of human carnage. Ruined several pairs of trousers. Nobody who has not been in the trenches can have the faintest conception of the horror of it. I had hardly set foot in France before I sank in up to the knees in a pair of twill jodphurs with pigskin straps handstitched by Ramidge and Hawkes. And so it went on – the sixteen ounce serge, the heavy worsteds, the silk flannel mixture – until I was invalided out with a bullet through the calf of an irreplaceable lambswool dyed khaki in the yarn to my own specification. I tell you, there is nothing in Switzerland to compare with it.

TZARA: Oh, come now, Henry, your trousers always look –

CARR: I mean with trench warfare.

TZARA: Well, I daresay, Henry, but you could have spent the time in Switzerland as an artist.

CARR (*Coldly*): My dear Tristan, to be an artist *at all* is like living in Switzerland during a world war. To be an artist *in Zurich, in 1917*, implies a degree of self-absorption that would have glazed over the eyes of Narcissus. When I sent round to Hamish and Rudge for their military pattern book, I was responding to feelings of *patriotism*, *duty*, to my love of freedom, my hatred of tyranny and my sense of oneness with the underdog – I mean in general, I never particularly cared for the Belgians as such. And besides I couldn't be an artist *anywhere* – I can do none of the things by which is meant Art.

TZARA: Doing the things by which is meant Art is no longer considered the proper concern of the artist. In fact it is frowned upon. Nowadays, an artist is someone who makes art mean the things he does. A man may be an artist by exhibiting his hindquarters. He may be a poet by drawing words out of a hat.

CARR: But that is simply to change the meaning of the word Art.

TZARA: I see I have made myself clear.

CARR: Then you are not actually *an artist* at all?

TZARA: On the contrary. I have just told you I am.

CARR: But that does not make you an artist. An artist is someone who is gifted in some way that enables him to do something more or less well which can only be done badly or not at all by someone who is not thus gifted. If there is any point in using language at all it is that a word is taken to stand for a particular fact or idea and not for other facts or ideas. I might claim to be able to fly . . . Lo, I say, I am flying. But you are not propelling yourself about while suspended in the air, someone may point out. Ah no, I reply, that is no longer considered the proper concern of people who can fly. In fact, it is frowned upon. Nowadays, a flyer never leaves the ground and wouldn't know how. I see, says my somewhat baffled interlocutor, so when you say you can *fly* you are using the word in a purely private sense. I see I have made myself clear, I say. Then, says this chap in some relief, you cannot actually *fly* after all? On the contrary, I say, I have just told you I can. Don't you see my dear Tristan you are simply asking me to accept that the word Art means whatever you wish it to mean; but I do not accept it.

TZARA: Why not? You do exactly the same thing with words like *patriotism, duty, love, freedom,* king and country, brave little Belgium, saucy little Serbia –

CARR: (*Coldly*): You are insulting my comrades-in-arms, many of whom died on the field of honour –

TZARA: – and honour – all the traditional sophistries for waging wars of expansion and self-interest, set to patriotic hymns.

Music is corrupted, language conscripted. Words are taken to stand for their opposites. That is why anti-art is the art of our time.

(*The argument becomes progressively more heated.*)

CARR: The nerve of it. Wars are fought to make the world safe for artists. It is never quite put in those terms but it is a useful way of grasping what civilized ideals are all about. The easiest way of knowing whether good has triumphed over evil is to examine the freedom of the artist. The *ingratitude* of artists, indeed their hostility, not to mention the loss of nerve and failure of talent which accounts for 'modern art', merely demonstrate the freedom of the artist to be ungrateful, hostile, self-centred and talentless, for which freedom I went to war.

TZARA: Wars are fought for oil wells and coaling stations; for control of the Dardanelles or the Suez Canal; for colonial pickings to buy cheap in and conquered markets to sell dear in. War is capitalism with the gloves off and many who go to war know it but they go to war because they don't want to be a hero. It takes courage to sit down and be counted. But how much better to live bravely in Switzerland than to die cravenly in France, quite apart from what it does to one's trousers.

CARR: My God, you little Romanian wog – you bloody dago – you jumped-up phrase-making smart-alecy arty-intellectual Balkan turd!!! Think you know it all! – while we poor dupes think we're fighting for ideals, you've got a profound understanding of what is *really* going on, underneath! – you've got a phrase for it! You pedant! Do you think your phrases are the true sum of each man's living of each day? – *capitalism with the gloves off?* – do you think that's the true experience of a wire-cutting party caught in a crossfire in no-man's-land? (*Viciously*) It's all the rage in Zurich! – You slug! I'll tell you what's *really* going on: I went to war because it was my *duty*, because my country needed me, and that's *patriotism*. I went to war because I believed that those boring little Belgians and incompetent Frogs had the right to be defended from German militarism, and that's *love of freedom. That's* how things are underneath, and I won't be told by some yellow-bellied Bolshevik that I ended up in the trenches because there's a profit in ball-bearings!

TZARA (*Storming*): *Quite right!* You ended up in the trenches, because on the 28th of June 1900 the heir to the throne of Austro-Hungary married beneath him and found that the wife he loved was never allowed to sit next to him on royal occasions, except! when he was acting in his military capacity as Inspector General of the Austro-Hungarian army – in which capacity he therefore decided to inspect the army in Bosnia, so that *at least on their wedding anniversary*, the 28th of June 1914, they might ride side by side in an open carriage through the streets of Sarajevo! (*Sentimentally*) Aaaaah! (*Then slaps his hands sharply together like a gun-shot*) Or, to put it another way –

CARR (*Quietly*): We're here because we're here . . . because we're here because we're here . . . we're here because we're here because we're here because we're here . . .

(CARR *has dropped into the familiar chant, quite quiet.*
TZARA *joins in, just using the sound 'da-da' to the same tune.
The light starts to go. The chant grows. When* CARR *starts to speak,* TZARA *continues the chanting quietly for a few more moments under* CARR's *words.*)

Great days! The dawn breaking over no-man's-land – Dewdrops glistening on the poppies in the early morning sun! The trenches stirring to life! . . . 'Good morning, corporal! All quiet on the Western Front?' . . . 'Tickety-boo, sir!' – 'Carry on!' – Wonderful spirit in the trenches – never in the whole history of human conflict was there anything to match the courage, the comradeship, the warmth, the cold, the mud, the stench – fear – folly – Christ Jesu!, but for this blessed leg! – I never thought to be picked out, plucked out, blessed by the blood of a blighty wound – oh *heaven!* – released into folds of snow-white feather beds, pacific civilian heaven!, the mystical swissticality of it, the entente cordiality of it!, the Jesus Christ I'm out of it! – into the valley of the invalided – Carr of the Consulate!

(*Lights to normal.*)

And what brings *you* here, my dear Tristan?

TZARA: Oh, pleasure, pleasure . . . What else should bring anyone anywhere? Eating as usual, I see, Henry?

CARR: I believe it is customary in good society to take a cucumber sandwich at five o'clock. Where have you been since last Thursday?

TZARA: In the Public Library.

CARR: What on earth were you doing there?

TZARA: That's just what I kept asking myself.

CARR: And what was the reply?

TZARA: 'Ssssh!' Cecily does not approve of garrulity in the Reference Section.

CARR: Who is Cecily? And is she as pretty and well-bred as she sounds? Cecily is a name well thought of at fashionable christenings.

TZARA: Cecily is a librarianness. I say, do you know someone called Joyce?

CARR: *Joyce* is a name which could only expose a child to comment around the font.

TZARA: No, no, Mr Joyce, Irish writer, mainly of limericks, christened James Augustine, though registered, due to a clerical error, as James Augusta, a little known fact.

CARR: Certainly I did not know it. But then I have never taken an interest in Irish affairs. In fashionable society it would be considered a sign of incipient vulgarity with radical undertones.

TZARA: The war caught Joyce and his wife in Trieste in Austro-Hungary. They got into Switzerland and settled in Zurich. He lives in Universitatsstrasse, and is often seen round about, in the library, in the cafés, wearing, for example, a black pinstripe jacket with grey herringbone trousers, or brown Donegal jacket with black pinstripe trousers, or grey herringbone jacket with brown Donegal trousers, all being the mismatched halves of sundry sundered Sunday suits: sorts language into hands of contract bridge. His limericks are said to be more interesting, though hardly likely to start a revolution – I say, do you know someone called Ulyanov?

CARR: I'm finding this conversation extremely hard to follow.

And you still have not told me what you were doing in the public library. I had no idea that poets nowadays were interested in literature. Or is it that your interest is in Cecily?

TZARA: Good heavens, no. Cecily is rather pretty, and well-bred, as you surmised, but her views on poetry are very old-fashioned and her knowledge of the poets, as indeed of everything else, is eccentric, being based on alphabetical precedence. She is working her way along the shelves. She has read Allingham, Anon, Arnold, Belloc, Blake, both Brownings, Byron, and so on up to, I believe, G.

CARR: Who is Allingham?

TZARA: 'Up the airy mountain, down the rushy glen, we daren't go a-hunting for fear of little men . . .' Cecily would regard any poem that came out of a hat with the gravest suspicion. Hello – why the extra cup? – why cucumber sandwiches? Who's coming to tea?

CARR: It is merely set for Gwendolen – she usually returns at about this hour.

TZARA: How perfectly delightful, and to be honest not unexpected. I am in love with Gwendolen and have come expressly to propose to her.

CARR: Well, that is a surprise.

TZARA: Surely not, Henry; I have made my feelings for Gwendolen quite plain.

CARR: Of course you have, my dear fellow. But my surprise stems from the fact that you must surely have met Gwendolen at the Public Library, for she has left here every morning this week saying that that is where she is going, and Gwendolen is a scrupulously truthful girl. In fact, as her elder brother I have had to speak to her about it. Unrelieved truthfulness can give a young girl a reputation for insincerity. I have known plain girls with nothing to hide captivate the London season purely by discriminate mendacity.

TZARA: Oh, I assure you Gwendolen has been in the Public Library. But I have had to admire her from afar, all the way from Economics to Foreign Literature.

CARR: I had no idea Gwendolen knew any foreign languages, and I am not sure that I approve. It's the sort of thing that can only broaden a girl's mind.

TZARA: Well, in this library Foreign Literature includes English.

CARR: What a novel arrangement. Is any reason given?

TZARA (*Impatiently*): The point is, Henry, I can't get to speak to her alone.

CARR: Ah, yes – her chaperone.

TZARA: Chaperone?

CARR: Yes – you don't imagine I'd let my sister go unchaperoned in a city largely frequented by foreigners. Gwendolen has made a friend in Zurich. I have not met her but Gwendolen assures me that they are continuously in each other's company, and from a description which I have elicited by discreet questioning she cannot but be a wholesome and restraining influence, being practically middle-aged, plainly dressed, bespectacled and answering to the name of Joyce, oh good heavens. Is he after her money?

TZARA: Only in derisory instalments. He claims to be writing a novel, and has made a disciple out of Gwendolen. She transcribes for him, looks things up in works of reference, and so on. The poor girl is so innocent she does not stop to wonder what possible book could be derived from reference to Homer's *Odyssey* and the Dublin Street Directory for 1904.

CARR: Homer's *Odyssey* and the Dublin Street Directory?

TZARA: For 1904.

CARR: I admit it's an unusual combination of sources, but not wholly without possibilities. Anyway, there's no need to behave as though you were married to her already. You are not married to her already, and I don't think you ever will be.

TZARA: Why on earth do you say that?

CARR: In the first place, girls never marry Romanians, and in the second place I don't give my consent.

TZARA: Your consent!

CARR: My dear fellow, Gwendolen is my sister and before I allow you to marry her you will have to clear up the whole question of Jack.

TZARA: Jack! What on earth do you mean? What do you mean,

Henry, by Jack? I don't know anyone of the name of Jack.

CARR (*Taking a library ticket from his pocket*): You left this here the last time you dined.

TZARA: Do you mean to say you have had my library ticket all this time? I had to pay a small fine in replacing it.

CARR: That was extravagant of you, since the ticket does not belong to you. It is made out in the name of Mr Jack Tzara, and your name isn't Jack, it's Tristan.

TZARA: No, it isn't, it's Jack.

CARR: You have always told me it was Tristan. I have introduced you to everyone as Tristan. You answer to the name of Tristan. Your notoriety at the Meierei Bar is firmly associated with the name Tristan. It is perfectly absurd saying your name isn't Tristan.

TZARA: Well, my name is Tristan in the Meierei Bar and Jack in the library, and the ticket was issued in the library.

CARR: To write – or at any rate to draw words out of a hat – under one name, and appear at the Public Library under another is an understandable precaution – but I cannot believe that that is the whole explanation.

TZARA: My dear Henry, the explanation is perfectly simple. One day last year, not long after the triumph at the Meierei Bar of our noise concert for siren, rattle and fire-extinguisher, a bunch of the boys were sinking a beer at the Cafe Zum Adler – myself, Hans Arp, Hugo Ball, Picabia . . . Arp, as usual, was inserting a warm croissant into his nose, I was quietly improving a Shakespeare sonnet with a pair of scissors.

CARR: Which one?

TZARA: I believe it was the Eighteenth, the one beginning
'Vergleichen solle ich dich dem Sommertag,
Da du weit lieblicher, weit milder bist?'

CARR: But surely, in German it's hardly worth the trouble.

TZARA (*Cheerfully*): Oh, completely pointless. If it weren't, it wouldn't be Dada. Well, who should come in but Ulyanov, also known as Lenin, with a group of Zimmerwaldists.

CARR: That sounds like the last word in revolutionary socialism.

TZARA: It is. At Zimmerwald in 1915 we called on the workers of the world to oppose the war.

CARR: We?

TZARA: Well, I dine with them, and, in fact, was doing so on this occasion when someone at the bar piano started to play a Beethoven sonata. Lenin went completely to pieces, wept like a child. When he recovered he dried his eyes and lashed into the Dadaists! – 'decadent nihilists, flogging too good for them', and so on. Fortunately, the name Tzara meant nothing to him, but a few days later I met him at the library and he introduced me to Cecily. 'Tzara!' said she. 'Not the Dadaist, I hope!' I could feel Lenin's eyes upon me. 'My younger brother, Tristan,' I replied. 'Most unfortunate. Terrible blow to the family.' When I filled up my application form, for some reason the first name I thought of was Jack. It has really turned out rather well.

CARR (*With great interest*): Cecily knows *Lenin*, does she?

TZARA: Oh, yes, he's made quite a disciple out of Cecily. She's helping him with his book on Imperialism.

CARR (*Thoughtfully*): Did you say the reference section?

TZARA: They agree on everything, including art. As a Dadaist, I am the natural enemy of bourgeois art and the natural ally of the political left, but the odd thing about revolution is that the further left you go politically the more bourgeois they like their art.

CARR: There's nothing odd about that. Revolution in art is in no way connected with *class* revolution. Artists are members of a privileged class. Art is absurdly overrated by artists, which is understandable, but what is strange is that it is absurdly overrated by everyone else.

TZARA: Because man cannot live by bread alone.

CARR: Yes, he can. It's *art* he can't live on. When I was at school, on certain afternoons we all had to do what was called Labour – weeding, sweeping, sawing logs for the boiler-room, that kind of thing; but if you had a chit from Matron you were let off to spend the afternoon messing about in the Art Room. Labour or Art. And you've got a chit for *life*? (*Passionately*) *Where did you get it?* What is an artist? For every thousand people there's nine hundred doing the work, ninety doing well, nine doing good, and one lucky bastard who's the artist.

TZARA (*Hard*): Yes, by Christ! – and when you see the drawings he made on the walls of the cave, and the fingernail patterns he one day pressed into the clay of the cooking pot, *then* you say, *My God, I am of these people!* It's not the hunters and the warriors that put you on the first rung of the ladder to consecutive thought and a rather unusual flair in your poncey trousers.

CARR: Oh yes it was. The hunter decorated the pot, the warrior scrawled the antelope on the wall, the artist came home with the kill. All of a piece. The idea of the artist as a special kind of human being is art's greatest achievement, and it's a fake!

TZARA: My God, you bloody English philistine – you ignorant smart-arse bogus bourgeois Anglo-Saxon prick! When the strongest began to fight for the tribe, and the fastest to hunt, it was the artist who became the priest-guardian of the magic that conjured the intelligence out of the appetites. Without him, man would be a coffee-mill. Eat – grind – shit. Hunt – *eat* – fight – *grind* – saw the logs – *shit*. The difference between being a man and being a coffee-mill is art. But that difference has become smaller and smaller and smaller. Art created patrons and was corrupted. It began to celebrate the ambitions and acquisitions of the pay-master. The artist has negated himself: paint – *eat* – sculpt – *grind* – write – *shit*. (*A light change.*)

Without art man was a coffee-mill: but *with* art, man – is a coffee-mill! That is the message of Dada. – dada dada dada dada dada dada dada dada dada dada dada dada dada dada . . .

(TZARA *is shouting, raving.* CARR *immobile.*)

(*Normal light as* BENNETT *opens the door. Everything back to 'normal'.*)

BENNETT: Miss Gwendolen and Mr Joyce.

(GWENDOLEN *and* JOYCE *appear as before.* BENNETT *retires.*)

JOYCE: Good morning, my name is James Joyce –

CARR: James Augusta?

JOYCE (*Taken aback*): Was that a shot in the dark?

CARR: Not at all – I am a student of footnotes to expatriate Irish literature.

JOYCE: You know my work?

CARR: No – only your name.

TZARA: Miss Carr . . .

GWEN: Mr Tzara . . .

CARR: . . . but something about you suggests Limerick.

JOYCE: Dublin, don't tell me you know it?

CARR: Only from the guidebook, and I gather you are in the process of revising that.

JOYCE: Yes.

GWEN: Oh! I'm sorry – how terribly rude! Henry – Mr Joyce –

CARR: How'dyou do?

JOYCE: Delighted.

TZARA: Good day.

JOYCE: I just wanted to say –

GWEN: Do you know Mr Tzara, the poet?

JOYCE: By sight, and reputation; but I am a martyr to glaucoma and inflation. Recently as I was walking down the Bahnhofstrasse my eye was caught by a gallery showcase and I was made almost insensible with pain.

GWEN: Mr Joyce has written a poem about it. It is something you two have in common.

JOYCE: Hardly. Mr Tzara's disability is monocular, and, by rumour, affected, whereas I have certificates for conjunctivitis, iritis and synechia, and am something of an international eyesore.

GWEN: I mean poetry. I was thinking of your poem 'Bahnhofstrasse', beginning
'The eyes that mock me sign the way
Whereto I pass at eve of day,
Grey way whose violet signals are
The trysting and the twining star.'

TZARA (*To* JOYCE): For your masterpiece
I have great expectorations
(GWEN's *squeak*, '*Oh!*')
For you I would evacuate a monument.
(*Oh!*)
Art for art's sake – I am likewise defecated

GWEN: Dedicated –

TZARA: I'm a foreigner.

JOYCE: So am I.

GWEN: But it is the most beautiful thing I've ever heard. I have
a good ear, would you not agree, Mr Tzara?

TZARA: It is the most perfect thing about you, Miss Carr.

GWEN: Oh, I hope not. That would leave no room for
development.

JOYCE: But have you not read any of Mr Tzara's poems?

GWEN: To my shame I have not – but perhaps the shame is
yours, Mr Tzara.

TZARA: I accept it – but the matter can be easily put right, and
at once.

GWEN (*Fluttering*): Oh, Mr Tzara! . . .
(TZARA *retires to the sideboard, or writing table if there is one,
and begins to write fluently on a large piece of white paper.*)

CARR (*To* JOYCE): And what about you, Doris?

JOYCE: Joyce.

CARR: Joyce.

JOYCE: It is not as a poet that I come to see you, sir, but as the
business manager of the English Players, a theatrical
troupe.

CARR: The business manager?

JOYCE: Yes.

CARR: Well, if it's money you want, I'm afraid . . .

GWEN: Oh, Henry! – he's mounting a play, and Mr Joyce
thought your official support –

JOYCE: Perhaps I'd better explain. It seems, sir, that my name is
in bad odour among the British community in Zurich.
Whether it is my occasional contribution to the neutralist
press, or whether it is my version of *Mr Dooley*, beginning:
'Who is the man, when all the gallant nations run to war,
Goes home to have his dinner by the very first cable car,
And as he eats his canteloupe contorts himself with mirth
To read the blatant bulletins of the rulers of the earth?'
– and ending:
'It's Mr Dooley
Mr Dooley
The wisest wight our country ever knew!

31

                 "Poor Europe ambles
                 like sheep to shambles"
                 Sighs Mr Dooley-ooley-ooley-ooo.'
or some other cause altogether, the impression remains that I
regard both sides with equal indifference.

CARR: And you don't?

JOYCE: Only as an artist. As an artist, naturally I attach no
importance to the swings and roundabout of political history.
But I come here not as an artist but as James A. Joyce. I am
an Irishman. The proudest boast of an Irishman is – I paid
back my way . . .

CARR: So it is money.

JOYCE: A couple of pounds would be welcome – certainly, but it
is to repay a debt that I have come. Not long ago, after many
years of self-reliance and hardship during which my work
had been neglected and reviled even to the point of being
burned by a bigoted Dublin printer, there being no other
kind of printer available in Dublin, I received £100 from the
Civil List at the discretion of the Prime Minister.

CARR: The Prime Minister –?

JOYCE: Mr Asquith.

CARR: I am perfectly well aware who the Prime Minister *is* – I am
the representative of His Majesty's Government in Zurich.

JOYCE: The Prime Minister is Mr Lloyd George, but at that time
it was Mr Asquith.

CARR: Oh yes.

JOYCE: I do not at this moment possess £100, nor was it the
intention that I would repay the debt in kind. However I
mentioned the English Players. By the fortune of war,
Zurich has become the theatrical centre of Europe. Here
culture is the continuation of war by other means – Italian
opera against French painting – German music against
Russian ballet – but nothing from England. Night after
night, actors totter about the raked stages of this alpine
renaissance, speaking in every tongue but one – the tongue of
Shakespeare – of Sheridan – of Wilde . . . The English
Players intend to mount a repertoire of masterpieces that will
show the Swiss who leads the world in dramatic art.

CARR: Gilbert and Sullivan – by God!

GWEN: And also Mr Joyce's own play *Exiles* which so far, unfortunately –

JOYCE: That's quite by the way –

CARR: *Patience!*

JOYCE: Exactly. First things first.

CARR: *Trial by Jury! Pirates of Penzance!*

JOYCE: We intend to begin with that quintessential English jewel, *The Importance of Being Earnest.*

CARR (*Pause*): I don't know it. But I've heard of it and I don't like it. It is a play written by an Irish – (*Glances at* GWENDOLEN) Gomorrahist – Now look here, Janice, I may as well tell you, His Majesty's Government –

JOYCE: I have come to ask you to play the leading role.

CARR: What?

JOYCE: We would be honoured and grateful.

CARR: What on earth makes you think that I am qualified to play the leading role in *The Importance of Being Earnest*?

GWEN: It was my suggestion, Henry. You were a wonderful Goneril at Eton.

CARR: Yes, I know, but –

JOYCE: We are short of a good actor to play the lead – he's an articulate and witty English gentleman –

CARR: Ernest?

JOYCE: Not Ernest – the other one.

CARR (*Tempted*): No – no – I absolutely –

JOYCE: Aristocratic – romantic – epigrammatic – he's a young swell.

CARR: A swell . . . ?

JOYCE: He says things like, I may occasionally be a little overdressed but I make up for it by being immensely over-educated. That gives you the general idea of him.

CARR: How many changes of costume?

JOYCE: Two complete outfits.

CARR: Town or country?

JOYCE: First one then the other.

CARR: Indoors or out?

JOYCE: Both.

33

CARR: Summer or winter?

JOYCE: Summer but not too hot.

CARR: Not raining?

JOYCE: Not a cloud in the sky.

CARR: But he could be wearing – a boater?

JOYCE: It is expressly stipulated.

CARR: And he's not in – pyjamas?

JOYCE: Expressly proscribed.

CARR: Or in mourning?

JOYCE: Not the other one – Ernest.

CARR (*Claps his hands once*): Describe the play briefly, omitting all but essential detail.

JOYCE: Act One. The curtain rises. A flat in Mayfair. Teatime. You enter in a bottle-green velvet smoking jacket with black frogging – hose white, cravat perfect, boots elastic-sided, trousers of your own choice. Act Two.

CARR: I shall have to make certain expenditures.

JOYCE: A rose garden. After lunch. Some by-play among the small parts. You enter in a debonair garden party outfit – beribboned boater, gaily striped blazer, parti-coloured shoes, trousers of your own choice.

CARR (*Instantly*): Cream flannel.

JOYCE: Act Three. The morning room. A few moments later.

CARR: A change of costume?

JOYCE: Possibly by the alteration of a mere line or two of dialogue . . .

CARR: You have brought a copy of the play?

JOYCE: I have it here.

CARR: Then let us retire to the next room and peruse it.

(CARR *opens the door of 'his' room for* JOYCE.)

JOYCE: About those two pounds –

CARR (*Generously, reaching for his wallet*): My dear Phyllis . . . !

(*– and closes it after them.*)

(*Pause. Freeze.*)

GWEN (*Absently*): Gomorrahist . . . Silly bugger.

(TZARA *comes forward with rare diffidence, holding a hat like a brimming bowl. It transpires that he has written down a Shakespeare sonnet and cut it up into single words which he has*

34

placed in the hat.)

TZARA: Miss Carr . . .

GWEN: Mr Tzara! – you're not leaving? (*The hat*)

TZARA: Not before I offer you my poem.

(*He offers the hat.* GWEN *looks into it.*)

GWEN: Your technique is unusual.

TZARA: All poetry is a reshuffling of a pack of picture cards, and
all poets are cheats. I offer you a Shakespeare sonnet, but it is
no longer his. It comes from the wellspring where my atoms
are uniquely organized, and my signature is written in the
hand of chance.

GWEN: Which sonnet – was it?

TZARA: The eighteenth. In English.

GWEN: 'Shall I compare thee to a summer's day . . .'
'. . . Thou art more lovely and more temperate.
Rough winds do shake the darling buds of May
And summer's lease hath all too short a date . . .'

(*And she continues accompanied by a romantic orchestra.*)
'Sometimes too hot the eye of heaven shines,
And often is his gold complexion dimm'd;
And every fair from fair sometime declines,
By chance or nature's changing course untrimm'd;
But thy eternal summer shall not fade
Nor lose possession of that fair thou owest;
Nor shall Death brag thou wander'st in his shade,
When in eternal lines to time thou growest:
So long as men can breathe or eyes can see,
So long lives this and this gives life to thee . . .'

TZARA: Yes, that's the one.

GWEN: You tear him for his bad verses?

(*She lets a handful of words fall from her fingers, back into the
hat, and her sadness starts to give way to anger.*)
These are but wild and whirling words, my lord.

TZARA: Ay, Madam.

GWEN: Truly I wish the gods had made thee poetical.

TZARA: I do not know what poetical is. Is it honest in word and
deed? Is it a true thing?

GWEN: Sure he that made us with such large discourse, looking before and after, gave us not *that* capability, *and* god-like reason to fust in us unused.

TZARA: I was not born under a rhyming planet. Those fellows of infinite tongue that can rhyme themselves into ladies' favours, they do reason themselves out again. And that would set my teeth nothing on edge – *nothing* so much as mincing poetry.

GWEN (*Rising to his vicious edge*): Thy honesty and love doth mince *this* matter – Put your bonnet for his right use, 'tis for the head! (*Sniffs away a tear*) I had rather than forty shilling I had my book of songs and sonnets here.

(*She has turned away. He approaches with his hat offered.*)

TZARA (*Gently*): But since he died, and poet better prove, his for his style you'll read, mine for my – love.

(GWEN *hesitates but then takes the first slip of paper out of the hat.*)

GWEN: 'Darling'.

(*She now continues, holding on to all the pieces of paper she takes out.*)

    shake thou thy gold buds
    the untrimm'd but short fair shade
    shines –
    see, this lovely hot possession growest
    so long
    by nature's course –
    so . . . long – heaven!

(*She gives a little shriek, using 'heaven' and turns her back on the hat, taking a few steps away from* TZARA, *who takes out the next few words, lowering the temperature . . .*)

TZARA: And declines,
    summer changing, more temperate complexion . . .

GWEN (*Still flustered*): Pray don't talk to me about the weather, Mr Tzara. Whenever people talk to me about the weather I always feel quite certain that they mean something else.

TZARA (*Coming to her*): I do mean something else, Miss Carr. Ever since I met you I have admired you.

(*He drops his few papers into the hat, she does likewise with hers, he puts the hat aside.*)

GWEN: For me you have always had an irresistible fascination. Even before I met you I was far from indifferent to you. As you know I have been helping Mr Joyce with his new book, which I am convinced is a work of genius. Alas, in fashionable society, genius is regarded as an affront to the ordinary decencies of family life. A girl has few opportunities to meet a man like yourself who shares her regard for Mr Joyce as an artist.

TZARA: I, Gwendolen?

GWEN: Did you think, my darling, that I had not noticed you at the library? – how you gaze at him in admiration all the way from Economics to Foreign Literature? When I elicited by discreet questioning that you, too, were a poet of the most up-to-date disposition, I knew I was destined to love you.

TZARA (*Amazed*): Do you really love me, Gwendolen?

GWEN: Passionately!

TZARA: Darling, you don't know how happy you've made me.

GWEN: My own Tristan!

(*They embrace.*)

TZARA (*Breaking off*): But you don't mean that you couldn't love me if I didn't share your regard for Mr Joyce as an artist?

GWEN: But you do.

TZARA: Yes. I know I *do*, but supposing –

(*She kisses him on the mouth.*)

(*They embrace.* JOYCE *re-enters.*)

JOYCE: Rise, sir, from that semi-recumbent posture!

(TZARA *and* GWEN *spring apart.* JOYCE *walks across to the main door, picking up his hat, opens the door, addresses* TZARA.) Your monocle is in the wrong eye.

(TZARA *has indeed placed his monocle in the wrong eye. He replaces it.* JOYCE *has left on his line.*)

GWEN: I must tell Henry!

(GWEN *gives* TZARA *the folder she acquired in the Prologue.*) Here is a chapter of Mr Joyce's book which I have been transcribing for him.

TZARA: But have you ever come across Dada, darling?

GWEN: Never, da-da-darling! The chapter we are doing next is cast in the form of the Christian Catechism!

37

(GWEN *kisses him and runs into Henry's room.*)
(*The main door opens again and* JOYCE *re-enters, pausing in the threshold. He is covered from head to breast in little bits of white paper, each bit bearing one of the words of Shakespeare's eighteenth sonnet, i.e.* TZARA *was using Joyce's hat.*)

JOYCE: What is the meaning of this?

TZARA: It has no meaning. It is without meaning as Nature is. It is Dada.

JOYCE: Give further examples of Dada.

TZARA: The Zoological Gardens after closing time. The logical gardenia. The bankrupt gambler. The successful gambler. The Eggboard, a sport or pastime for the top ten thousand in which the players, covered from head to foot in eggyolk, leave the field of play.

JOYCE: Are you the inventor of this sport or pastime?

TZARA: I am not.

JOYCE: What is the name of the inventor?

TZARA: Arp.

JOYCE: By what familiarity, indicating possession and amicability in equal parts, do you habitually refer to him?

TZARA: My friend Arp.

JOYCE: Alternating with what colloquialism redolent of virtue and longevity?

TZARA: Good old Arp.

JOYCE: From whom did Arp receive encouragement and friendship?

TZARA: From Hugo Ball.

JOYCE: Describe Ball by epithet.

TZARA: Unspherical. Tall, thin, sacerdotal, German.

JOYCE: Describe him by enumeration of his occupations and preoccupations.

TZARA: Novelist, journalist, philosopher, poet, artist, mystic, pacifist, founder of the Cabaret Voltaire at the Meierei Bar, number one Spiegelgasse.

JOYCE: Did Ball keep a diary?

TZARA: He did.

JOYCE: Was it published?

TZARA: It was.

JOYCE: Is it in the public domain by virtue of the expiration of copyright protection as defined in the Berne Convention of 1886?

TZARA: It is not.

JOYCE: Quote discriminately from Ball's diary in such a manner as to avoid forfeiting the goodwill of his executors.

TZARA: 'I went to the owner of the Meierei Bar and said, "I want to start a nightclub." That same evening Tzara gave a reading of poems, conservative in style, which he rather endearingly fished out of the various pockets of his coat.'

JOYCE: Is that the coat?

TZARA: It is.

JOYCE: In what regard is a coat inferior, and in what superior, to a hat in so far as they are interchangeable in the production of poetry?

TZARA: *Inferior* to a hat in regard to the tendency of one or both sleeves to hang down in front of the eyes, with the resultant possibility of the wearer falling off the edge of the platform. *Superior* to a hat in regard to the number of its pockets.

JOYCE: Amplify discreetly from any contemporary diarist whose estate is not given to obsessive litigation over trivial infringements of copyright.

TZARA: 'On February 26th Richard Huelsenbeck arrived from Berlin, and on March 30th Herr Tristan Tzara was the initiator of a performance, the first in Zurich and in the world, of simultanist verse, including a poème simultané of his own composition.'

JOYCE: Quote severally your recollections of what was declaimed synchronously.

TZARA: I began, 'Boum boum boum il déshabille sa chair quand les grenouilles humides commencerent a brûler.' Huelsenbeck began, 'Ahoi ahoi des admirals gwirktes Beinkleid schnell zerfallt.' Janco chanted, 'I can hear the whip o' will around the hill and at five o'clock when tea is set I like to have my tea with some brunette, everybody's doing it, doing it.' The title of the poem was 'Admiral Seeks House To Let'.

(*All this time,* JOYCE *has been picking bits of paper from his hair*

39

and from his clothes, replacing each bit in his hat, which is on his knees. Casually, he conjures from the hat a white carnation, apparently made from the bits of paper (he turns the hat up to show it is empty). He tosses the carnation at TZARA.)

JOYCE: How would you describe this triumph?

TZARA (*Putting the carnation into his buttonhole*): As just and proper. Well merited. An example of enterprise and charm receiving their due.

(JOYCE *starts to pull silk hankies from the hat.*)

JOYCE: What, reduced to their simplest reciprocal form, were Tzara's thoughts about Ball's thoughts about Tzara, and Tzara's thoughts about Ball's thoughts about Tzara's thoughts about Ball?

TZARA: He thought that he thought that he knew what he was thinking, whereas he knew that he knew that he knew that he did not.

JOYCE: And did he?

TZARA: He did and he didn't.

JOYCE: What did Dada bring to pictorial art, sculpture, poetry and music that had not been brought to these activities previously in . . .

(*The appropriate flags start coming out of the hat.*)

. . . Barcelona, New York, Paris, Rome and St Petersburg by, for example, Picabia, Duchamp, Satie, Marinetti, and Mayakovsky who shouts his fractured lines in a yellow blazer with blue roses painted on his cheeks?

TZARA: The word Dada.

JOYCE: Describe sensibly without self-contradiction, and especially without reference to people stuffing bread rolls up their noses, how the word Dada was discovered.

TZARA: Tristan Tzara discovered the word Dada by accident in a Larousse Dictionary. It has been said, and he does not deny, that a paper-knife was inserted at random into the book. Huelsenbeck recounts how *he* discovered the word one day in Hugo Ball's dictionary while Tzara was not present. Hans Arp, however, has stated, 'I hereby declare that Tristan Tzara found the word Dada on February the 8th 1916 at six o'clock in the afternoon.'

JOYCE: Were there further disagreements between Tzara and Huelsenbeck?

TZARA: There were.

JOYCE: As to?

TZARA: As to the meaning and purpose of Dada.

JOYCE: Huelsenbeck demanding, for example?

TZARA: International revolutionary union of all artists on the basis of radical Communism.

JOYCE: As opposed to Tzara's demanding?

TZARA: The right to urinate in different colours.

JOYCE: Each person in different colours at different times, or different people in each colour all the time? Or everybody multi-coloured every time?

TZARA: It was more to make the point that making poetry should be as natural as making water –

JOYCE (*Rising: the conjuring is over*): God send you don't make them in the one hat.

(*This is too much for* TZARA.)

TZARA: By God, you supercilious streak of Irish puke! You four-eyed, bog-ignorant, potato-eating ponce! Your art has failed. You've turned literature into a religion and it's as dead as all the rest, it's an overripe corpse and you're cutting fancy figures at the wake. It's too late for geniuses! Now we need vandals and desecrators, simple-minded demolition men to smash centuries of baroque subtlety, to bring down the temple, and thus finally, to reconcile the shame and the necessity of being an artist! Dada! *Dada! Dada!!*

(*He starts to smash whatever crockery is to hand; which done, he strikes a satisfied pose.* JOYCE *has not moved.*)

JOYCE: You are an over-excited little man, with a need for self-expression far beyond the scope of your natural gifts. This is not discreditable. Neither does it make you an artist. An artist is the magician put among men to gratify – capriciously – their urge for immortality. The temples are built and brought down around him, continuously and contiguously, from Troy to the fields of Flanders. If there is any meaning in any of it, it is in what survives as art, yes even in the celebration of tyrants, yes even in the celebration of nonentities. What now of the Trojan War if it had been passed over by the artist's touch? Dust. A forgotten expedition prompted by Greek merchants looking for new markets. A minor redistribution of broken pots. But it is we who stand enriched, by a tale of heroes, of a golden apple, a wooden horse, a face that launched a thousand ships – and above all, of Ulysses, the wanderer, the most human, the most complete of all heroes – husband, father, son, lover, farmer, soldier, pacifist, politician, inventor and adventurer ... It is a theme so overwhelming that I am almost afraid to treat it. And yet I with my Dublin Odyssey will double that immortality, yes by God *there's* a corpse that will dance for some time yet and *leave the world precisely as it finds it* – and if you hope to shame it into the grave with your fashionable magic, I would strongly advise you to try and acquire some genius and if possible some subtlety before the season is quite over. Top o' the morning, Mr Tzara!

(*With which* JOYCE *produces a rabbit out of his hat, puts the hat on his head, and leaves, holding the rabbit.*)

(CARR'*s voice is heard off.*)

CARR (*Voice off*): 'Really, if the lower orders don't set us a good example what on earth is the use of them? They seem as a class to have absolutely no sense of moral responsibility.'

(TZARA *has moved to* CARR'*s door. He opens it, and goes through.*)

(*Voice off*) 'How are you, my dear Ernest. What brings you up to town?' – 'Pleasure, pleasure – eating as usual, I see, Algy . . .'

(CARR *enters, as Old Carr, holding a book.*)

Algy! The other one. Personal triumph in the demanding role of Algernon Montcrieff. The Theater zur Kaufleuten on Pelikanstrasse, an evening in Spring, the English Players in that quintessential English jewel 'The Imprudence of Being –' Now I've forgotten the first one. By Oscar Wilde. Henry Carr as Algy. Other parts played by Tristan Rawson, Cecil Palmer, Ethel Turner, Evelyn Cotton . . . forget the rest. Tickets five francs, four bob a nob and every seat filled, must have made a packet for the Irish lout and his cronies – still,

not one to bear a grudge, not after all these years, and him
dead in the cemetery up the hill, unpleasant as it is to be
dragged through the courts for a few francs – after I'd paid
for my trousers *and* filled every seat in the house – *not* very
pleasant to be handed ten francs like a *tip*! – and then asking
me for twenty-five francs for tickets – bloody nerve – Here, I
got it out –

(*From his pocket, a tattered document.*)

– Bezirksgericht Zuerich, Zurich District Court, in the case
of Dr James Joyce – doctor my eye – plaintiff and counter-
defendant versus Henry Carr, defendant and counter-
plaintiff, with reference to the claim for settlement of the
following issues: (a) Suit: is defendant and counter-plaintiff
(that's me) obliged to pay the plaintiff and counter-defendant
(that's him) twenty-five francs? (b) Counter-suit: is plaintiff
and counter-defendant bound to pay defendant and counter-
plaintiff three hundred francs? Have you got that? Joyce says
I owe him twenty-five francs for tickets. I say Joyce owes me
three hundred francs for the trousers, etcetera, purchased by
me for my performance as Henry – or rather – *god dammit!* –
the other one . . .

Incidentally, you may or may not have noticed that I got
my wires crossed a bit here and there, you know how it is
when the old think-box gets stuck in a groove and before you
know where you are you've jumped the points and suddenly
you think, No, steady on, old chap, that was Algernon –
Algernon! There you are – all coming back now, I've got it
straight, I'll be all right from here on. In fact, anybody
hanging on just for the cheap comedy of senile confusion
might as well go because now I'm on to how I met Lenin and
could have changed the course of history etcetera, what's
this?? (*the document*) Oh yes.

Erkannt – has decided that. 1. Der Beklagte, the
defendant, Henry Carr, is obliged to pay den Klager, the
plaintiff, James Joyce, twenty-five francs. The counter-claim
of Henry Carr is denied. Herr Carr to indemnify Doktor
Joyce sixty francs for trouble and expenses. In other words, a
travesty of justice. Later the other case came up – Oh yes, he

sued me for slander, claimed I called him a swindler and a cad . . . Thrown out of court, naturally. But it was the money with Joyce. Well, it was a long time ago. He left Zurich after the war, went to Paris, stayed twenty years and turned up here again in December 1940. Another war . . . But he was a sick man then, perforated ulcer, and in January he was dead . . . buried one cold snowy day in the Fluntern Cemetery up the hill.

I dreamed about him, dreamed I had him in the witness box, a masterly cross-examination, case practically won, admitted it all, the whole thing, the trousers, everything, and I *flung* at him – 'And what did you do in the Great War?' 'I wrote *Ulysses*,' he said. 'What did you do?'

Bloody nerve.

(BLACKOUT.)

ACT TWO

Apart from the bookcases, etc. the Library's furniture includes
CECILY's *desk, which is perhaps more like a counter forming three*
sides of a square.
CECILY: To resume.

The war caught Lenin and his wife in Galicia, in Austro-
Hungary. After a brief internment they got into Switzerland
and settled in Berne. In 1916, needing a better library than
the one in Berne, Lenin came to Zurich . . .
(The Library set is now lit.)
. . . intending to stay two weeks. But he and Nadezhda liked
it here and decided to stay. They rented a room in the house
of a shoe-maker named Kammerer at 14 Spiegelgasse.
Zurich during the war was a magnet for refugees, exiles,
spies, anarchists, artists and radicals of all kinds. Here could
be seen James Joyce, reshaping the novel into the permanent
form of his own monument, the book the world now knows
as *Ulysses!* – and here, too, the Dadaists were performing
nightly at the Cabaret Voltaire in the Meierei Bar at Number
One Spiegelgasse, led by a dark, boyish and obscure
Romanian poet . . .
(JOYCE is seen passing among the bookshelves; and also CARR,
now monocled and wearing blazer, cream flannels, boater . . .
and holding a large pair of scissors which he snips speculatively
as he passes between the bookcases. JOYCE *and* CARR *pass out of*
view.)
Every morning at nine o'clock when the library opened,
Lenin would arrive.
(LENIN arrives, saying 'Good morning' in Russian:
'Zdrasvuitiye'.)
He would work till the lunch hour, when the library closed,
and then return and work until six, except on Thursdays
when we remained closed. He was working on his book on
Imperialism.

45

(LENIN *is at work among books and papers.*)
On January 22nd, 1917, at the Zurich People's House Lenin told an audience of young people, 'We of the older generation may not live to see the decisive battles of the coming revolution.' We all believed that that was so. But one day hardly more than a month later, a Polish comrade, Bronsky, ran into the Ulyanov house with the news that there was a revolution in Russia . . .
(NADYA *enters as in the Prologue, and she and* LENIN *repeat the Russian conversation previously enacted. This time* CECILY *translates it for the audience, pedantically repeating each speech in English, even the simple 'No!' and 'Yes!' The* LENINS *leave.* NADYA *says 'Das vedanya' to* CECILY (*i.e. 'Goodbye') as she goes.*)
As Nadezhda writes in her *Memories of Lenin*, 'From the moment the news of the February revolution came, Ilyich burned with eagerness to go to Russia.' But this was easier said than done, in this landlocked country. Russia was at war with Germany. And Lenin was no friend of the Allied countries. His war policy made him a positive danger to them;
(CARR *enters, very debonair in his boater and blazer, etc.* CARR *has come to the library as a 'spy', and his manner betrays this until* CECILY *addresses him.*)
indeed it was clear that the British and the French would wish to prevent Lenin from leaving Switzerland. And that they would have him watched. Oh!
(CECILY *sees* CARR *who hands her the visiting card he received from* BENNETT *in Act One.*)
CECILY: Tristan Tzara. Dada, Dada, Dada . . . *Why, it's Jack's younger brother!!*
CARR: You must be Cecily!
CECILY: Ssssh!
CARR: You are!
CECILY: And you, I see from your calling card, are Jack's decadent nihilist younger brother.
CARR: Oh, I'm not really a decadent nihilist at all, Cecily. You mustn't think that I am a decadent nihilist.

CECILY: If you are not then you have certainly been deceiving us all in a very inexcusable manner. To *masquerade* as a decadent nihilist – or at any rate to ruminate in different colours and display the results in the Bahnhofstrasse – would be hypocritical.

CARR: (*Taken aback*): Oh! Of course, I have been rather *louche* and devil-take-the-hindmost.

CECILY: I am glad to hear it.

CARR: In fact now you mention the subject I have made quite a corner in voluptuous disdain.

CECILY: I don't think you should be so proud of it, however pleasant it must be. You have been a great disappointment to your brother.

CARR: Well, my brother has been a great disappointment to me, and to Dada. His mother isn't exactly mad about him either. My brother Jack is a booby, and if you want to know why he is a booby, I will tell you why he is a booby. He told me that you were rather pretty, whereas you are at a glance the prettiest girl in the whole world. Have you got any books here one can borrow?

CECILY: I don't think you ought to talk to me like that during library hours. However, as the reference section is about to close for lunch I will overlook it. Intellectual curiosity is not so common that one can afford to discourage it. What kind of books were you wanting?

CARR: Any kind at all.

CECILY: Is there no limit to the scope of your interests?

CARR: It is rather that I wish to increase it. An overly methodical education has left me to fend as best I can with some small knowledge of the aardvark, a mastery of the abacus and a facility for abstract art. An aardvark, by the way, is a sort of African pig found mainly –

CECILY: I know only too well what an aardvark is, Mr Tzara. To be frank, you strike a sympathetic chord in me.

CARR: Politically, I haven't really got beyond anarchism.

CECILY: I see. Your elder brother, meanwhile –

CARR: Bolshevism. And you, I suppose . . .?

CECILY: Zimmervaldism!

CARR: Oh, Cecily, will you not make it your mission to reform me? We can begin over lunch. It will give me an appetite. Nothing gives me an appetite so much as renouncing my beliefs over a glass of hock.

CECILY: I'm afraid I am too busy to reform you today. I must spend the lunch hour preparing references for Lenin.

CARR: Some faithful governess seeking fresh pastures?

CECILY: Far from it. I refer to Vladimir Ilyich who with my little help is writing his book on 'Imperialism, the highest stage of capitalism'.

CARR: Of course – *Lenin*. But surely, now that the revolution has broken out in St Petersburg, he will be anxious to return home.

CECILY: That is true. When the history of the Revolution – or indeed of anything else – is written, Swizterland is unlikely to loom large in the story. However, all avenues are closed to him. He will have to travel in disguise with false papers. Oh, but I fear I have said too much already. Vladimir is positive that there are agents watching him and trying to ingratiate themselves with those who are close to him. The British are among the most determined, though the least competent. Only yesterday the Ambassador received secret instructions to watch the ports.

CARR (*Ashamed*): The ports?

CECILY: At the same time, the Consul in Zurich has received a flurry of cryptic telegrams suggesting intense and dramatic activity – 'Knock 'em cold' – 'Drive 'em Wilde' – 'Break a leg' – and one from the Ambassador himself, 'Thinking of you tonight, Horace.'

CARR: I think I can throw some light on that. The Consul has been busy for several weeks in rehearsals which culminated last evening in a performance at the Theater zur Kaufleuten on Pelikanstrasse. I happened to be present.

CECILY: That would no doubt explain why he virtually left the Consulate's affairs in the hands of his manservant – who, fortunately, has radical sympathies.

CARR: Good heavens!

CECILY: You seem surprised.

CARR: Not at all. I have a servant myself.

CECILY: I am afraid that I disapprove of servants.

CARR: You are quite right to do so. Most of them are without scruples.

CECILY: In the socialist future, no one will have any.

CARR: So I believe. To whom did this manservant pass the Consul's correspondence?

CECILY: Your brother Jack. Oh dear, there I go again! You are not a bit like your brother. You are more English.

CARR: I assure you I am as Bulgarian as he is.

CECILY: He is Romanian.

CARR: They are the same place. Some people call it the one, some the other.

CECILY: I didn't know that, though I always suspected it.

CARR: Anyway, now that *Earnest* has opened, no doubt the Consul will relieve his servant of diplomatic business. In all fairness, he did have a personal triumph in a most demanding role.

CECILY: *Earnest??*

CARR: No – the other one.

CECILY: What do you mean by *Earnest*?

CARR: *The Importance of Being Earnest* by Oscar Wilde.

CECILY: Wilde?

CARR: You know him?

CECILY: No, in literature I am only up to G. But I've heard of him and I don't like him. The life is the art, as Vladimir Ilyich always says.

CARR: Ars longa, vita brevis, Cecily.

CECILY: Let us leave his proclivities in the decent obscurity of a learned tongue, Mr Tzara. I was referring to the fact that Oscar Wilde was a bourgeois individualist and, so I hear, overdressed from habit to boot.

CARR: From habit to boot?

CECILY: And back again.

CARR: He may occasionally have been a little over-dressed but he made up for it by being immensely uncommitted.

CECILY: The sole duty and justification for art is social criticism.

CARR: That is a most interesting view of the sole duty and

justification for art, Cecily, but it has the disadvantage that a great deal of what we call art has no such function and yet in some way it gratifies a hunger that is common to princes and peasants.

CECILY: In an age when the difference between prince and peasant was thought to be in the stars, Mr Tzara, art was naturally an affirmation for the one and a consolation to the other; but we live in an age when the social order is seen to be the work of material forces and we have been given an entirely new kind of responsibility, the responsibility of changing society.

CARR: No, no, no, no, no – my dear girl! – art doesn't change society, it is merely changed by it.

(*From here the argument becomes gradually heated.*)

CECILY: Art is a critique of society or it is nothing!

CARR: Do you know Gilbert and Sullivan??!

CECILY: I know Gilbert but not Sullivan.

CARR: Well, if you knew *Iolanthe* like I know *Iolanthe* –

CECILY: I doubt it –

CARR: *Patience!*

CECILY: How dare you!

CARR: *Pirates! Pinafore!*

CECILY: Control yourself!

CARR: *Ruddigore!*

CECILY: This is a Public Library, Mr Tzara!

CARR: *GONDOLIERS, Madam!*

(*Another 'time slip . . .'*)

CECILY: I don't think you ought to talk to me like that during library hours. However as the reference section is about to close for lunch I will overlook it. Intellectual curiosity is not so common that one can afford to discourage it. What kind of books were you wanting?

CARR: Any kind at all. You choose. I should like you, if you would, to make it your mission to reform me. We can begin over lunch.

CECILY: I'm afraid I am too busy to reform you today. You will have to reform yourself. Here is an article which I have been translating for Vladimir Ilyich. You may not be aware, Mr

Tzara, that in the governments of Western Europe today there are ten Socialist ministers.

CARR: I must admit my work has prevented me from taking an interest in European politics. But ten is certainly impressive.

CECILY: It is scandalous. They are supporting an imperialist war. Meanwhile the real struggle, the class war, is being undermined by these revisionists like Kautsky and MacDonald.

CARR (*Puzzled*): Do you mean Ramsay MacDonald, Cecily?

CECILY: I don't mean Flora Macdonald, Mr Tzara.

CARR: But he's an absolute Bolshie.

CECILY: He is working within the bourgeois capitalist system and postponing its destruction. Karl Marx has shown that capitalism is digging its own grave.

CARR: No, no, no, no, my dear girl – Marx got it wrong. He got it wrong for good reasons but he got it wrong just the same. By bad luck he encountered the capitalist system at its most deceptive period. The industrial revolution had crowded the people into slums and enslaved them in factories, but it had not yet begun to bring them the benefits of an industrialized society. Marx drew the lesson that the wealth of the capitalist had been stolen from the worker in the form of unpaid labour. He thought that was how the whole thing worked. That false premise was itself added to a false assumption. Marx assumed that people would behave according to their class. But they didn't. In all kinds of ways and for all kinds of reasons, the classes moved closer together instead of further apart. The critical moment never came. It receded. The tide must have turned at about the time when *Das Kapital* after eighteen years of hard labour was finally coming off the press, a moving reminder, Cecily, of the folly of authorship. How sweet you look suddenly – pink as a rose.

CECILY: That's because I'm about to puke into your nancy straw hat, you *prig*! – you swanking canting fop, you bourgeois intellectual humbugger, you – *artist*! Marx warned us against the liberals, the philanthropists, the piecemeal reformers – change won't come from *them* but from a head-on collision, *that's* how history works! When Lenin was 21 there was

51

famine in Russia. The intellectuals organized relief – soup kitchens, seed corn, all kinds of do-gooding with Tolstoy in the lead. Lenin did – nothing. He understood that the famine was a force for the revolution. Twenty-one years old, in Samara, in 1890–91. He was a boy, and he understood that, so don't talk to me about superior morality, you patronizing Kant-struck prig, all the time you're talking about the classes you're trying to imagine how I'd look stripped off to my knickers –

CARR: That's a lie!

(*But apparently it isn't. As* CECILY *continues to speak we get a partial Carr's-mind view of her. Coloured lights begin to play over her body, and most of the other light goes except for a bright spot on Carr.*)

(*Faintly from 1974, comes the sound of a big band playing* 'The Stripper'. CARR *is in a trance. The music builds.* CECILY *might perhaps climb on to her desk. The desk may have 'cabaret lights' built into it for use at this point.*)

CECILY: The only way is the way of Marx and of Lenin, the enemy of all revisionism! – of opportunist liberal economism! – of social-chauvinist bourgeois individualism! – quasi-Dadaist paternalism! – pseudo-Wildean aphorism! – sub-Joycean catechism and dogmatism! – cubism! – expressionism! – rheumatism! –

CARR: *Get 'em off!*

(*The light snaps back to normal.*)

CECILY: I don't think you ought to talk to me like that during library hours. However, as the reference section is about to close for lunch I will overlook it. Intellectual curiosity is not so common that one can afford to discourage it. What kind of books were you wanting?

CARR: Books? What books? What do you mean, Cecily, by books? I have read Mr Lenin's article and I don't need to read any more. I have come to tell you that you seem to me to be the visible personification of absolute perfection.

CECILY: In body or mind?

CARR: In every way.

CECILY: Oh, Tristan!

CARR: You will love me back and tell me all your secrets, won't you?

CECILY: You silly boy! Of course! I have waited for you for months.

CARR (*Amazed*): For months?

CECILY: Ever since Jack told me he had a younger brother who was a decadent nihilist it has been my girlish dream to reform you and to love you.

CARR: Oh, Cecily!

(*Her embrace drags him down out of sight behind her desk. He resurfaces momentarily –*)

CARR: But, my dear Cecily, you don't mean that you couldn't love me if –

(*– and is dragged down again.*)

(*NADYA enters, wearing a bonnet, severely dressed and carrying a book . . .*)

NADYA: From the moment news of the revolution came, Ilyich burned with eagerness to go to Russia . . . He did not sleep and at night all sorts of incredible plans were made.

(*LENIN enters, wearing a clerical collar, but otherwise dressed in black from parson's hat to parson's leggings. He and NADYA look at each other and despair – Chasuble and Prism.*)

But such things could only be thought of in the semi delirium of the night.

(*NADYA takes off her bonnet. LENIN takes off his hat and removes his clerical collar.*)

A passport of a foreigner from a neutral country would have to be obtained.

LENIN (*Dictating to* NADYA): Letter to Yakov Ganetsky in Stockholm, March 19th, 1917.

(*NADYA writes on a pad.*)

'I cannot wait any longer. No legal means of transit available. Whatever happens, Zinoviev and I must reach Russia. The only possible plan is as follows: you must find two Swedes who resemble Zinoviev and me, but since we cannot speak Swedish they must be deaf mutes. I enclose our photographs for this purpose.'

(*CARR, with his jacket off, surfaces from behind Cecily's desk.*)

CARR: Two Swedish deaf mutes . . . ??

(An unseen hand yanks him back out of sight.)

NADYA: The plan mentioned in this letter was not realized.

(LENIN produces a blonde wig from a cardboard box and puts the wig on his head.)

(Writing in her pad) Letter to V. A. Karpinsky in Geneva, the same day, March 19th, 1917.

LENIN *(Dictating)*: 'My dear Vyacheslav Alexeyevich. I am considering carefully and from every point of view what will be the best way of travelling to Russia. The following is absolutely secret.'

(For emphasis, LENIN bangs his fist inadvertently on the bell on Cecily's desk. CECILY pops up and disappears again without being seen by LENIN.)

'Please procure in your name papers for travelling to France and England. I will use these when passing through England and Holland to Russia. I can wear a wig. The passport photograph will be of me in a wig. I shall go to the Berne Consulate to present your papers and I shall be wearing the wig.'

(CARR reappears again, fully dressed, and eavesdrops on the LENINS.)

(Continuing) 'You must disappear from Geneva for at least two or three weeks, until you receive a telegram from me in Scandinavia . . . Your Lenin. P.S.: I write to you because I am convinced that everything between us will remain *absolutely* secret.'

(TZARA enters briskly, unseen by CARR and not seeing him, and bangs the bell on Cecily's desk. CECILY pops up from behind the desk.)

CECILY: Jack?

TZARA *(Turning away)* Cecily!

CECILY: I have such a surprise for you. Your brother is here.

TZARA: What nonsense! I haven't got a brother.

(He turns the other way and sees CARR) – Oh my God.

(The LENINS stop and stare at these events.)

CARR: Brother Jack, I have come to tell you that I am sorry for all the embarrassment I have caused you in the past, and that I hope very much that I do not have to embarrass you in the future.

CECILY: Jack, you are not going to refuse your own brother's hand!

TZARA: Nothing will induce me to take his hand. He knows perfectly well why.

CECILY: Jack, if you don't shake hands with your brother I'll never forgive you.

TZARA: Well, don't forgive me. Why should I care? The fact of the matter is, he is no more my –
(*At this point* LENIN *removes his wig and* TZARA *recognizes him.*)
Ah . . . Comrade! Do you know my brother Tristan?
(CARR *shakes hands heartily with the stunned* LENINS. CARR *holds his hand out to* TZARA.)

CARR: How do you do Comrade, Mrs Comrade. Brother!

TZARA (*Shaking hands*): This is the last time I shall ever do it.

CECILY: How pleasant it is to see so perfect a reconciliation. Let us leave the two brothers together.

NADYA: The plan mentioned in this letter was not realized.
(*The* LENINS *gather their possessions and leave,* CECILY *going with them.*)

CARR: She is a darling. I am in love with Cecily. Which puts me in something of a moral dilemma. I must have a muffin to resolve it. You can have some tea-cake.
(*The library gives way to Carr's room, the conversation continuing.*)

TZARA: But I don't like tea-cake. Besides, I have sworn never to shake hands with you again.

CARR: I don't want you to shake hands with me when I'm eating muffins. Muffins should never be eaten with shaking hands.
(*As* BENNETT *enters with a muffin dish*)
Ah, Bennett. Is there anything in my correspondence that I might share with you and Mr Tzara?

BENNETT: The odds on Lenin have shortened somewhat, sir, but you can still get a hundred to one against.

CARR: A hundred to one?

TZARA: Put a tenner on for me, would you, Bennett? – running the show by Christmas.

CARR: And a tenner for me, Bennett – the dustbin of history.

BENNETT: Yes, sir.

(BENNETT *leaves.* CARR *and* TZARA *help themselves to the contents of the dish.*)

TZARA: I am shocked, Henry. You are surely not going to let your so-called duty stand in the way of your love for Cecily Carruthers.

CARR: I haven't decided – there are still several muffins left.

(*He takes one.* NADYA *enters, dressed to travel, and lugging a suitcase and a bundle or two. The boundary between Library and Room is now, perhaps, obscure.*)

NADYA: On the same day, March 19th, there was a meeting of the Russian political emigré groups in Switzerland to discuss ways and means of getting back to Russia. Martov suggested obtaining permits to pass through Germany in exchange for German and Austrian prisoners of war interned in Russia.

(LENIN *enters, similarly dressed and similarly encumbered.*)

LENIN: March 21st, letter to Karpinsky in Geneva. 'Martov's plan is good. Only, we cannot deal directly with the German authorities.'

NADYA: Therefore, Comrade Grimm, President of the Zimmerwald Committee, undertook the negotiations. March 25th – telegram from the German High Command to the Foreign Ministry in Berlin. 'No objection to the transit of Russian revolutionaries if effected in special train with reliable escort.'

CARR: (*Eating a muffin*): Look – be fair. I adore Cecily, but the Americans are about to enter the war and it's not a good moment for some Bolshevik to pull the Russians out of it. It could turn the whole thing round. I mean, I *am* on the side of right. Remember plucky little Poland – not Poland, the other one.

LENIN: Our tactics – no trust in and no support of the new Government. Kerensky especially suspect. Arming of the proletariat is the only guarantee. Telegraph this to St Petersburg.

CARR: Mind you, according to Marx, the dialectic of history will get you to much the same place with or without Lenin. If Lenin did not exist, it would be unnecessary to invent him.

LENIN: Telegram to Ganetsky in Stockholm. 'Twenty of us are leaving tomorrow.'

CARR: Furthermore, your Marxism is sheer pretension. You're an amiable bourgeois with a chit from matron and if the revolution came you wouldn't know what hit you. You're nothing. You're an artist. And multi-coloured micturition is no trick to those boys, they'll have you pissing blood.

TZARA: Artists and intellectuals will be the conscience of the revolution. It is perfectly heartless of you to eat all the muffins and leave me with tea-cakes.

NADYA: On April 9th, at 2.30 in the afternoon, the travellers moved off from the Zahringer Hof Restaurant in true Russian style, loaded with pillows, blankets and a few personal belongings. Ilyich wore a bowler hat, a heavy overcoat and the thick-soled hobnailed boots that had been made for him by the cobbler Kammerer at number 14 Spiegelgasse. Telegram to his sister in St Petersburg:

LENIN: 'Arriving Monday night, eleven. Tell Pravda.'

TZARA (*Getting up*): Well, do what you will. To a Dadaist history comes out of a hat too.

CARR: I don't think there'll be a place for Dada in a Communist society.

TZARA: That's what we have against this one. There's a place for us in it!

(TZARA *leaves*.)

NADYA: The train left at 3.10, on time.

(LENIN *and* NADYA *leave with their luggage. Sound of train departing.*)

(*The train is heard, and perhaps seen, to leave.* CECILY *appears, dressed for the station platform, and waves a red handkerchief at the departing train.*)

CARR (*Decisively*): No, it is perfectly clear in my mind. He must be stopped. The Russians have got a government of patriotic and moderate men. Prince Lvov is moderately conservative, Kerensky is moderately socialist, and Guchkov is a businessman. All in all a promising foundation for a liberal democracy on the Western model, and for a vigorous prosecution of the war on the Eastern front, followed by a

57

rapid expansion of trade. I shall telegraph the Minister in Berne.

(CARR *leaves. Everything black except a light on* LENIN. *There is a much reproduced photograph of Lenin addressing the crowd in a public square in May 1920 – 'balding, bearded, in the three-piece suit', as Carr describes him; he stands as though leaning into a gale, his chin jutting, his hands gripping the edge of the rostrum which is waist-high, the right hand at the same time gripping a cloth cap . . . a justly famous image.*)

(LENIN, *as the orator, is now the only person on stage.*)

LENIN (*Declaiming*): Really, if the lower orders don't set us a good example what on earth is the use of them?! They seem as a class to have absolutely no sense of moral responsibility! To lose one revolution is unfortunate. To lose two would look like carelessness!

(OLD CARR *enters, interrupting, consulting a tattered book.*)

OLD CARR (*Entering*): No, steady on – sorry – did you notice? Of course you did. Hello, hello, you thought, he's doing it again. Right – well, never mind, here's the picture. April 16th, Lenin in St Petersburg, yours truly holding the bag. I'd got pretty close to him, had a stroke of luck with a certain little lady and I'd got a pretty good idea of his intentions, in fact I might have stopped the whole Bolshevik thing in its tracks, but – here's the point. I was *torn*. On the one hand, the future of the civilized world. On the other hand, my feelings for Cecily. And, don't forget, *he wasn't Lenin then*! I mean, *who was he?*, as it were. There I was, the lives of millions of people hanging on which way I'd move or whether I'd move at all, another man might have cracked – sorry about that muffin business, incidentally. Be that as it may, where were we? Ah yes. (CARR *opens his book, searching in it.*) – Lenin on Literature and Art –

(CARR *remains on stage with the book.* LENIN *makes a fresh start.*)

LENIN: Today, literature must become party literature. Down with non-partisan literature! Down with literary supermen! Literature must become a part of the common cause of the proletariat, a cog in the Social democratic mechanism.

Publishing and distributing centres, bookshops and reading rooms, libraries and similar establishments must all be under party control. We want to establish and we shall establish a free press, free not simply from the police, but also from capital, from careerism, and what is more, free *from bourgeois anarchist individualism*!

(NADYA *enters with a copy of the same book.*)

NADYA (*Entering*): Ilyich wrote those remarks in 1905 during the first Revolution.

LENIN (*Continuing*): Everyone is free to write and say whatever he likes, without any restrictions. *But* every voluntary association, including the party, is also free to expel members who use the name of the party to advocate anti-party views. Secondly, we must say to you bourgeois individualists that your talk about absolute freedom is sheer hypocrisy. There can be no real and effective freedom in a society based on the power of money. Socialist literature and art will be free because the idea of socialism and sympathy with the working people, instead of greed and careerism, will bring ever new forces to its ranks!

(*The light goes out on* LENIN.)

CARR: And a lot more like that, but there's a bit somewhere about bosh and nonsense – hang on – (*He searches through the book.*)

NADYA: Ilyich wrote very little about art and literature, generally, but he enjoyed it. We sometimes went to concerts and the theatre, even the music hall – he laughed a lot at the clowns – and he was moved to tears when he saw *La Dame aux Camélias* in London in 1907.

CARR (*Sentimentally*): Oh . . . *La Dame aux Camélias* . . .

NADYA: Ilyich admired Tolstoy, especially *War and Peace*, but, as he put it in an article in 1908 on Tolstoy's eightieth birthday . . .

(LENIN *enters to join* NADYA)

LENIN (*Entering*): On the one hand we have the great artist; on the other hand we have the landlord obsessed with Christ. On the one hand the strong and sincere protester against social injustice, and on the other hand the jaded hysterical sniveller known as the Russian intellectual beating his breast in public and wailing, I am a bad wicked man, but I am practising moral self-perfection. I don't eat meat, I now eat rice cutlets. Tolstoy reflected the stored-up hatred and the readiness for a new future – and at the same time the immature dreaming and political flabbiness which was one of the main causes for the failure of the 1905 revolution.'

CARR (*Finding the place*): Here we are.

NADYA: However, he respected Tolstoy's traditional values. The *new* art seemed somehow alien and incomprehensible to him. Clara Zetkin, in her memoirs, remembers him bursting out –

CARR & LENIN: Bosh and nonsense!

LENIN: We are good revolutionaries but we seem to be somehow obliged to keep up with modern art. Well, as for me I'm a barbarian.

CARR & LENIN: Expressionism, futurism, cubism . . . I don't understand them and I get no pleasure from them.

CARR: That's my point. There was nothing wrong with Lenin except his politics.

LENIN: September 15, 1919, to A. M. Gorki, Dear Alexei Maximych . . . 'I recall a remark of yours during our talks in London, on Capri, and later – namely: "We artists are irresponsible people."'

CARR & LENIN (*Simultaneously*) Exactly!

LENIN: 'You utter incredibly angry words – about what? About a few dozen (or perhaps even a few hundred) Cadet and near-Cadet gentry spending a few days in jail in order to prevent plots which threaten the lives of tens of thousands of workers and peasants. A calamity indeed. What an injustice! A few days, or even weeks, in jail for intellectuals in order to prevent the massacre of tens of thousands of workers and peasants. "Artists are irresponsible people!"'

CARR: In other words, a chit from matron.

LENIN: 'Both on Capri and afterwards, I told you – you allow yourself to be surrounded by the very worst elements of bourgeois intelligentsia and succumb to their whining. No, really, you will go under if you don't tear yourself away from these bourgeois intellectuals. With all my heart I wish that you do this quickly. All the best. Yours, Lenin. P.S. For you are not writing anything!'

NADYA: Once in 1919 we went to a concert in the Kremlin and an actress started declaiming something by Mayakovsky. Mayakovsky was celebrated even before the revolution, when he used to shout his fractured lines in a yellow blazer with blue roses painted on his cheeks. Ilyich was in the front row, and he nearly jumped out of his skin.

LENIN: Memo to A. V. Lunacharsky, Commissar for Education – 'Aren't you ashamed for printing 5,000 copies of Mayakovsky's new book? It is nonsense, stupidity, double-dyed stupidity and affectation.'

CARR (*Simultaneously*): . . . 'Nonsense, stupidity, double-dyed stupidity and affectation.'

LENIN: 'Mayakovsky should be whipped for his Futurism.'

CARR: Mayakovsky shot himself in 1930. Tzara got fat and died in Paris in 1963. With modern art, you see, you have to pick your time and place.

NADYA: I remember when we were in London in 1903 how Ilyich longed to go to the Moscow Art Theatre to see *The Lower Depths*. We did so after the revolution. Well, the over-acting irritated him. After seeing *The Lower Depths* he avoided the theatre for a long time. But once we went to see *Uncle Vanya* which he liked very much. And finally the last time we went to the theatre, in 1922, we saw a stage version of Charles Dickens's *Cricket on the Hearth*. After the first act Ilyich found it dull. The saccharine sentimentality got on his nerves, and during the conversation between the old toy-maker and his blind daughter he could stand it no longer and we left.

(*The Appassionata Sonata of Beethoven is quietly introduced.*
CARR *closes his book and sighs.*)

CARR: Yes, I would have enjoyed a crack with Old Vladimir Ilyich – talking about art and literature in the cafés, strolling along the Bahnhofstrasse discussing Tolstoy and Dosty – the other one. It wasn't the same with Tzara and Joyce – never hit it off with them, never saw eye to eye. But Lenin and I . . . if only I'd known! But he had a train to catch and then it was too late. Pity. (*He goes upstage.*)

61

NADYA: But I remember him one evening, at a friend's house in
Moscow, listening to a Beethoven Sonata . . .

LENIN: I don't know of anything greater than the Appassionata.
Amazing, superhuman music. It always makes me feel,
perhaps naively, it makes me feel proud of the miracles that
human beings can perform. But I can't listen to music often.
It affects my nerves, makes me want to say nice stupid things
and pat the heads of those people who while living in this vile
hell can create such beauty. Nowadays we can't pat heads or
we'll get our hands bitten off. We've got to *hit* heads, hit
them without mercy, though ideally we're against doing
violence to people . . . Hm, one's duty is infernaliy hard . . .
(CARR *leaves the Room.* LENIN *leaves the Library. The music
continues.*)

NADYA: Once when Vladimir was in prison – in St Petersburg –
he wrote to me and asked that at certain times of day I should
go and stand on a particular square of pavement on the
Shpalernaya. When the prisoners were taken out for exercise
it was possible through one of the windows in the corridor to
catch a momentary glimpse of this spot. I went for several
days and stood a long while on the pavement there. But he
never saw me. Something went wrong. I forget what.
(*The Appassionata swells in the dark.*)
(*The Room:* GWEN *is seated. There are tea things on the table.
The Appassionata degenerates absurdly into 'Mr Gallagher and
Mr Shean'.* BENNETT *enters, followed by* CECILY. *The rhyme-
scheme of the song is fairly evident. The verses are of ten lines
each, the first line being a non-rhyming primer.*)

BENNETT: Miss Carruthers . . .

CECILY: Cecily Carruthers . . .

GWEN: Cecily Carruthers! What a pretty name!
             According to the Consul
             'Round the fashionable fonts you'll
             often hear the Cecily's declaimed.

CECILY: Oh dear Miss Carr, oh dear Miss Carr,
             pleasure remain exactly where you are –
             I beg you don't get up –

GWEN: (*To* BENNETT) I think we'll need another cup –
          Pray sit down, Miss Carruthers,
CECILY: So kind of you, Miss Carr.
     (*Exit* BENNETT.)
GWEN: Miss Carruthers, oh Miss Carruthers . . .
          I hope that you will call me Gwendolen.
          I feel I've known you long
          And I'm never ever wrong –
          Something tells me that we're going to be great
                                              friends.
CECILY: (*Upper class*) Oh Gwendolen! Oh, Gwendolen!
          It sounds ez pretty *ez* a mendolen!
          I hope that you'll feel free
          to call me Cecily . . .
GWEN: Absolutely, Cecily.
CECILY: Then that's settled Gwendolen.
CECILY: Oh Gwendolen, Oh, Gwendolen . . .
          I fear you don't remember where we met.
          I'm not so picturesque
          when seen behind a desk –
GWEN: Of *course*, my dear – *how* could I forget?
          Oh, Cecily, Oh, Cecily,
          Accept my sincere apology!
          Now be absolutely frank,
          is there trouble at the bank?
CECILY: At the Libr'ry, Gwendolen.
GWEN: At the *Libr'ry*, Cecily!

CECILY: Oh Gwendolen, Oh Gwendolen . . .
          I dread to state the reason for my call.
          The fact is there's a fee
          due on Homer's *Odyssey*
          and the *Irish Times* for June 1904.
GWEN: Oh Cecily, Oh Cecily,
          A friend of mine is writing *Ulysses*!
          I'm sure he never knew
          that the books were overdue –

CECILY: Since October, Gwendolen.

GWEN: On my ticket, Cecily!

(*Enter* BENNETT *with cup. There is a certain amount of tea-pouring and tea-sipping to come, not to mention the cup suddenly clinked down on the saucer, and all that; but directions to this effect are omitted.*)

GWEN: Oh Cecily, Oh Cecily . . .
     Aren't you the girl who has that Russian friend?
     I pass him every day
     by Economics A to K –

CECILY: (*Sadly*) It's never going to be the same again.
     Oh Gwendolen, Oh Gwendolen!
     He left this afternoon on the three-ten.
     I've just come from the train.
     But we'll hear of him again . . .

GWEN: (*Insincerely*) Absolutely, Cecily . . .

CECILY: *Positively*, Gwendolen!

(*Exit* BENNETT.)

CECILY: Oh Gwendolen, Oh Gwendolen . . .
     The Library is going to seem so sad.
     Apart from Mr Tzara
     all the Bolsheviki are a-
     board that special choo-choo bound for Petrograd.

GWEN: Excuse me, Cecily, dear Cecily . . .
     This Mr Tzara, does he spell it with a T?
     T-Z-A-R-A?
     A Bolshevik, you say?

CECILY: Absolutely, Gwendolen.

GWEN: You surprise me, Cecily

GWEN: Oh Cecily, oh Cecily . . .
     I must admit you've taken me aback.
     I shall certainly insist on
     a tête-à-tête with Tristan –

CECILY: With Tristan? – No, I mean his brother Jack.
     Oh Gwendolen, Oh Gwendolen!
     Tristan's quite another thing again.

GWEN: Brother Jack is news to me –

64

CECILY: They kept it in the family –
GWEN: Relatively, Cecily.
CECILY: Imminently, Gwendolen.

CECILY: Oh Gwendolen, Oh Gwendolen
            I'd like you to be the first to know . . .
            Tristan's hanging up his hat
            for the proletariat.
            We have an understanding –
GWEN: (*Rising*)   Just a mo-
            (*Sitting*) ment, Cecily, dear Cecily,
            Tristan's understanding is with me.
            What he writes (or draws)
            is no concern of yours.
CECILY: Relatively, Gwendolen –
GWEN: *Absolutely*, Cecily!
GWEN: Oh, Cecily . . . Oh Cecily . . .
            you have made an unfortunate mistake.
            Forgive me if I say
            (*Producing her diary*)
            Tristan mentioned yesterday
            he delectates his art for its own sake.
CECILY: Oh Gwendolen, Oh Gwendolen
            Clearly he has changed his mind since then.
            (*Producing her diary*)
            Today he said, 'My heart's
            no longer in the arts
            excepting, Cecily, as a means towards an end.'

GWEN: (*Frigid*) Oh Cecily, Oh Cecily . . .
            To say this gives me physical distress
            but one of Joyce's chapters
            sent Tristan into raptures
            on the subject of the stream of consciousness.
CECILY: Oh Gwendolen, Oh Gwendolen,
            it harrows me to contradict a friend,
            but his consciousness of class
            is the one that's going to last –

65

GWEN: Lower middle, Cecily?
CECILY: Are you really, Gwendolen?

GWEN: (*Rising*) Miss Carruthers,
CECILY: (*Ditto*)   Yes, Miss Carr.
GWEN: I do not wish to trespass on your time.
CECILY: I hope that I will see
         you at the Library
         should you ever get around to pay your fine.
         Miss Carr. (*Bows.*)
     (*To the door.*)
GWEN: Miss Carruthers,
         Is it done to wish you luck with all the others?
         I'm not awfully au fait
         with manners down your way –
CECILY: And up yours, Miss Carr – *Tristan!*
     (CARR *has entered. Pause.*)
GWEN: (*Censoriously*)   That's my brother.
CECILY: Your brother?
GWEN: Yes. My brother, Henry Carr.
CECILY: Do you mean that he is not Tristan Tzara the artist?
GWEN: Quite the contrary. He is the British Consul.
     (CARR *has frozen like a hunting dog. He is holding the folder
     given to him by* CECILY *in the Library.* BENNETT *opens the
     door.*)
BENNETT: Mr Tzara . . .
     (TRISTAN *enters.* BENNETT *retires.* TZARA *carries his folder.*)
GWEN: Tristan! My Tristan!
CECILY: Comrade Jack!
GWEN: Comrade Jack?
CECILY: Yes. The gentleman who has his arm round your waist is
     a luminary of the Zimmerwald Left.
GWEN: Are they Bolsheviks?
CECILY: Well, they dine with us.
GWEN: A gross deception has been practised upon us. My poor
     wounded Cecily!
CECILY: My sweet wronged Gwendolen!
     (*They are making for the door.*)

66

CECILY (*Halting*): There is just one question I should like to ask Mr Carr.

GWEN: An admirable idea. Mr Tzara, there is a question I should like to put to you.

CECILY: What in truth *was* your opinion of the essay I gave you to read?

GWEN: What indeed *did* you think of the chapter I showed you?

CARR (*Timidly*): Very . . . well written . . . Interesting style . . .

TZARA (*Timidly*): Very . . . well read . . . Rich material.

CECILY: But as a social critique –?

GWEN: But as art for art's sake –?

CARR (*Giving up*): *Rubbish!* He's a madman!

TZARA: Bilge! It's unreadable!

GWEN & CECILY: Oh! Hypocrites!

CARR: I'm sorry! 'Twas for love!

GWEN & CECILY: For love?

GWEN: That is true . . .

CECILY: Yes, it is.

    (*In unison they move towards the men, then in unison change their minds.*)

GWEN & CECILY: But our intellectual differences are an insuperable barrier!

    (*The door closes behind them.*)

    (CARR *and* TZARA *sink into the two main chairs.*)

CARR: By the way, I hear that Bennett has been showing you my private correspondence.

    (BENNETT *enters with champagne for two on a tray. He begins to dispense it.*)

TZARA: He has radical sympathies.

CARR: There is no one so radical as a manservant whose freedom of the champagne bin has been interfered with.

TZARA: So I believe.

CARR: Well, I've put a stop to it.

TZARA: Given him notice?

CARR: Given him more champagne.

TZARA: We Romanians have much to learn from the English.

CARR: I expect you'll be missing Sofia.

TZARA: You mean Gwendolen.

CARR (*Frowns; clears*): Bucharest.

TZARA: Oh, yes. Yes. The Paris of the Balkans . . .

CARR: Silly place to put it, really . . . (*Sips*) Is this the Perrier-
Jouet, Brut, '89????!!!

BENNETT: No, sir.

CARR (*He has read the writing on the wall*): *All gone . . . ?*

BENNETT (*Implacably*): I'm afraid so, sir.

CARR: Very well, Bennett.

BENNETT: I have put the newspapers and telegrams on the
sideboard, sir.

CARR: Anything of interest?

BENNETT: The *Neue Zuricher Zeitung* and the *Zuricher Post*
announce respectively the cultural high and low point of the
theatrical season at the Theater zur Kaufleuten yesterday
evening. The *Zeitung* singles you out for a personal triumph
in a demanding role. The Minister telegraphs his
congratulations, and also thanks you for your telegram to
him. He urges you to prevent Mr Ulyanov leaving
Swizterland at all costs.

(BENNETT *leaves*. PAUSE.)

CARR: Irish lout . . .

TZARA: Russian . . .

CARR: No – whatsisname – Deidre.

TZARA: Bridget . . . (*pause*)

CARR: Joyce!

TZARA: Joyce!

CARR: Lout. Quadri-oculate Irish git . . . Came round to the
dressing room and handed me ten francs like a *tip* – bloody
nerve – Sponger –

(BENNETT *enters*.)

BENNETT: Mr Joyce.

(JOYCE *enters in an agitated state*.)

JOYCE: Where is your sister?

CARR: Her money is in trust.

JOYCE: I have only one request to make of *you* –

CARR: And I have only one request to make of *you* – *why for God's
sake cannot you contrive just once to wear the jacket that is
suggested by your trousers??*

68

(*It is indeed the case that* JOYCE *is now wearing the other halves of the outfit he wore in Act One*.)

JOYCE (*With dignity*): If I could do it once, I could do it every time. My wardrobe got out of step in Trieste, and its reciprocal members pass each other endlessly in the night. Now – could you let me have the twenty-five francs.

CARR: What twenty-five francs?

JOYCE: You were given eight tickets to sell at five francs per ticket. My books indicate that only fifteen francs has been received from you.

CARR: I have spent three hundred and fifty francs of my own money so that your off-the-peg production should boast one character who looked as if he was acquainted with a tailor. If you hope to get a further twenty-five francs out of me you will have to drag me through the courts. (*Deliberately*) *You are a swindler and a cad!*

TZARA (*Handing* JOYCE *his folder*): Furthermore, your book has much in common with your dress. As an arrangement of words it is graceless without being random; as a narrative it lacks charm or even vulgarity; as an experience it is like sharing a cell with a fanatic in search of a mania.

(GWEN *and* CECILY *enter.* JOYCE *is scanning the manuscript.*)

JOYCE: Who gave you this manuscript to read?

GWEN: I did!

JOYCE: Miss Carr, did I or did I not give you to type a chapter in which Mr Bloom's adventures correspond to the Homeric episode of the Oxen of the Sun?

GWEN: Yes, you did! And it was wonderful!

JOYCE: Then why do you return to me an ill-tempered thesis purporting to prove, amongst other things, that Ramsay MacDonald is a bourgeois lickspittle gentleman's gentleman?

GWEN: (Aaaah)

TZARA: (Ohhhh)

CECILY: (Oops!)

CARR: (Aaah!)

JOYCE (*Thunders*): Miss Carr, where is the missing chapter???

CARR: Excuse me – did you say Bloom?

JOYCE: I did.

CARR: And is it a chapter, inordinate in length and erratic in style, remotely connected with midwifery?

JOYCE: It is a chapter which by a miracle of compression, uses the gamut of English literature from Chaucer to Carlyle to describe events taking place in a lying-in hospital in Dublin.

CARR (*Holding out his folder*): It is obviously the same work.

(GWEN *and* CECILY *swap folders with cries of recognition.* CARR *and* TZARA *close in. A rapid but formal climax, with appropriate cries of* 'Cecily! Gwendolen! Henry! Tristan!' *and appropriate embraces.*)

(*Music, appropriate to the period. Light change. A formal, short dance sequence.* TZARA *dances with* GWEN, CARR *with* CECILY. JOYCE *and* BENNETT *dance independently. The effect is of course a complete dislocation of the play.* CARR *and* CECILY *dance out of view. The others continue, and then they, too, dance offstage just as* OLD CARR *dances back on stage with* OLD CECILY.

(OLD CECILY *is about 80 of course, like Old Carr. They dance a few decrepit steps.*)

OLD CECILY: No, no, no, no it's pathetic though there was a court case I admit, and your trousers came into it, I don't deny, but you never got close to Vladimir Ilyich, and I don't remember the other one. I do remember Joyce, yes you are quite right and he was Irish with glasses but that was the year after – 1918 – and the train had long gone from the station! I waved a red hanky and cried long live the revolution as the carriage took him away in his bowler hat and yes, I said yes when you asked me, but he was the leader of millions by the time you did your Algernon . . .

CARR: Algernon – that was him.

OLD CECILY: I said that was the year after –

CARR: After what?

OLD CECILY: You never even saw Lenin.

CARR: Yes I did. Saw him in the cafés. I knew them all. Part of the job.

OLD CECILY: And you were never the Consul.

CARR: Never said I was.

OLD CECILY: Yes you did.

CARR: Should we have a cup of tea?

OLD CECILY: The Consul was Percy somebody.

CARR: (Bennett.)

OLD CECILY: What?

CARR (*Testily*): I said the Consul's name was Bennett!

OLD CECILY: Oh yes . . . Bennett . . . That's another thing –

CARR: *Are we going to have a cup of tea or not?*

OLD CECILY: And I never helped him write *Imperialism, the Highest Stage of Capitalism.* That was the year before, too. 1916.

CARR: Oh, Cecily. I wish I'd known then that you'd turn out to be a pedant! (*Getting angry*) Wasn't this – Didn't do that – 1916 – 1917 – *What of it?* I was here. They were here. They went on. I went on. We all went on.

OLD CECILY: No, we didn't. We stayed. Sophia married that artist. I married you. You played Algernon. They all went on.

(*Most of the fading light is on* CARR *now.*)

CARR: Great days . . . Zurich during the war. Refugees, spies, exiles, painters, poets, writers, radicals of all kinds. I knew them all. Used to argue far into the night . . . at the Odeon, the Terrasse . . . I learned three things in Zurich during the war. I wrote them down. Firstly, you're either a revolutionary or you're not, and if you're not you might as well be an artist as anything else. Secondly, if you can't be an artist, you might as well be a revolutionary . . .

    I forget the third thing.

(BLACKOUT.)